AF327909

KNOWINGNESS

KNOWINGNESS

The Second Volume of Quotations from the works of

L. RON HUBBARD

Bridge PUBLICATIONS, INC.

A HUBBARD PUBLICATION

Published in the United States by
Bridge Publications, Inc.
4751 Fountain Avenue
Los Angeles, California 90029

ISBN 0-88404-719-9

Important Note

In reading this book, be very certain you never go past a word you do not fully understand.

The only reason a person gives up a study or becomes confused or unable to learn is because he or she has gone past a word that was not understood.

The confusion or inability to grasp or learn comes AFTER a word that the person did not have defined and understood.

Have you ever had the experience of coming to the end of a page and realizing you didn't know what you had read? Well, somewhere earlier on that page you went past a word that you had no definition for or an incorrect definition for.

Here's an example. "It was found that when the crepuscule arrived the children were quieter and when it was not present, they were much livelier." You see what happens. You think you don't understand the whole idea, but the inability to understand came entirely from the one word you could not define, crepuscule, which means twilight or darkness.

It may not only be the new and unusual words that you will have to look up. Some commonly used words can often be misdefined and so cause confusion.

This datum about not going past an undefined word is the most important fact in the whole subject of study. Every subject you have taken up and abandoned had its words which you failed to get defined.

Therefore, in studying this book be very, very certain you never go past a word you do not fully understand. If the material becomes confusing or you can't seem to grasp it, there will be a word just earlier that you have not understood. Don't go any further, but go back to BEFORE you got into trouble, find the misunderstood word and get it defined.

Definitions

As an aid to the reader, words most likely to be misunderstood have been defined in the glossary at the back of this book. Words sometimes have several meanings. The definitions used in this glossary only give the meaning that the word has as it is used in the text. Other definitions for the word can be found in a dictionary.

Knowingness itself
is certainty.

Editors' Foreword

This collection of quotations has been designed especially for the Scientologist. It contains passages assembled from a broad selection of L. Ron Hubbard's writings and recorded lectures, categorized and indexed for ease of reading and reference.

Mr. Hubbard's writing is both powerful and poetic. Yet the full beauty of these words lies not only in the craftsmanship with which they were composed, but in the truths about ability, mankind and life which they impart.

As he stated in an article entitled "My Philosophy,"

"I know no man who has any monopoly upon the wisdom of this universe. It belongs to those who can use it to help themselves and others.

"If things were a little better known and understood, we would all lead happier lives."

We invite you not just to read the concepts outlined on these pages, but to use them.

—The Editors

Contents

On Knowingness

Knowing how to know is the definition of the highest level of knowingness.

The Philadelphia Doctorate Course Lectures

*The thetan is a knowingness,
total in a cleared state,
who yet can create space
and time and objects
to locate in them.
He reduces his knowingness
only to have action.*

The Creation of Human Ability

*K*nowingness
is being certainness.
One is as certain
as he can communicate.
He can communicate
as well as he can be.

Scientology 8-8008

*T*o obtain a certainty
one must be able to observe.

A New Slant on Life

*A*ll unknown is,
is out of communication.
All known is,
is in communication.

The Power of Simplicity Lectures

*K*nowingness is reduced
by assuming that one cannot know
or knows wrongly.

The Creation of Human Ability

*It is the unknown incident
which is the aberrative incident.
If the preclear knows about it,
it isn't aberrative.*

The Power of Simplicity Lectures

*Anxiety, indecision, uncertainty,
a state of "maybe" can exist only
in the presence of poor observation
or the inability to observe.*

A New Slant on Life

*Fear is a state of imperception,
fear is an unwillingness to confront.*

Personal Achievement Series Lecture: "Deterioration of Liberty"

*Knowingness is reduced
by assuming one must be
in certain places
to perceive and so know,
and that one cannot be
in certain places.*

The Creation of Human Ability

Perception is knowing across a distance.

Universes and the War Between Theta and MEST Lectures

The mechanics of perception consist of putting something out there and then wondering what it is.

Universes and the War Between Theta and MEST Lectures

Luck is chance.
To depend upon luck
is to depend upon not-knowingness.

The Problems of Work

It's part of wisdom to know
what you don't know.
And a man is only wise
who also knows what he doesn't know.
But he's stupid to say
that he can't know about something
or that something is unknowable.

Lecture: "The Field of Scientology"

$\mathcal{P}$ersonal integrity
is knowing what you know—
What you know
is what you know—
And to have the courage
to know and say
what you have observed.
And that is integrity
And there is no other integrity.

Article: "Personal Integrity"

The whole business of knowingness
is beingness.
If you can be something
you can certainly know it;
if you know something
you can certainly be it.

The Route to Infinity Lectures

*Increased awareness
is the only factor
which offers any road out.*

*That is an awfully simple truth,
but you'll find out
that people don't know that.
They think that less awareness
is the road out—and that is
the road down into the basement.*

Technical Bulletin: "The Big Auditing Problem"

If one can confront,
   he can be aware.

If he is aware,
   he can perceive and act.

If he can't confront,
   he will not be aware of things
      and will be withdrawn
      and not perceiving.

Thus he is unaware
   of things around him.

Technical Bulletin: "Confront"

*The essence of true knowledge
is the essence of existing
so that one can create beingness
and data to know.*

Scientology 8-8008

Those who gave us mystic
were sadistic.

The Route to Infinity Lectures: Appendix, "Dianetics Jingles"

*It should never be considered
by anyone
or under any circumstances
that anything which can affect him
could be beyond his ability to know
the full nature
of what he is experiencing.
If any lesson is contained in Scientology,
it is the lesson
that the gates to all knowingness
are open.*

Scientology 8-8008

On Education

Education which invites
and stimulates reason
and seeks to accelerate the individual
toward a successful and happy
level of existence,
and has enough faith in individuals
to assume the good usage of the education,
raises the individual on the Tone Scale.

Science of Survival

*A datum
or a formula
or anything like that
is really just as good to an individual
as it's workable.*

The Philadelphia Doctorate Course Lectures

*All things are complex
when they are poorly understood.*

Handbook for Preclears

The evolution of knowledge is toward simplicity, not complexity.

Handbook for Preclears

*Any knowledge
which can be sensed,
measured,
experienced,
by any entity
is capable of influencing that entity.*

The Philadelphia Doctorate Course Lectures

When a man tries to erect
the plans of a lifetime
or a profession
on data which he, himself,
has never evaluated,
he cannot possibly succeed.

A New Slant on Life

*Beginning to know
that one doesn't know
is not a lesson in humbleness
but one in wisdom.*

Personal Achievement Series Lecture:
"Differences Between Scientology and Other Studies"

*T**here is no knowledge*
worth knowing
that's in your memory bank.
All the knowledge
that's worth knowing
is outside your memory bank—
in complete and perfect contact
with the beingness that is you.

The Route to Infinity Lectures

$\mathcal{D}$ata is your data
only so long
as you have evaluated it.

Article: *"How to Study Scientology"*

*I*t is necessary
    that one be able to create,
        to receive,
    to know and to not-know
        information, data and thoughts.
Lacking any one of these skills,
    for they are skills,
        no matter how native
            they are to the individual,
one is apt to get into a chaos
    of thinkingness or creatingness
    or livingness.

Scientology: The Fundamentals of Thought

*It is difficult
   to be responsible for something
   or control something
unless you have knowledge of it.*

Management Series: "The Top Triangle"

As a society declines,
it more and more
resorts to authoritarian teaching
and attempts increasingly
to impress upon the individual
that he must adjust
to his environment
and that he cannot adjust
his environment to him.

*The educational process
becomes one of semihypnotically
receiving doughy masses of data
and regurgitating them
upon examination papers.
Reason and self-determinism
are all but forbidden.*

Science of Survival

The person being "educated" is, day after day, immobilized, made into an effect by instructors and denied original thought. He becomes a habitual "effect" and ceases to cause.

Handbook for Preclears

Life was busy teaching
somebody a lesson,
    and the lesson it succeeded
    in teaching him
was not to do any more living;
and that ultimate lesson, then,
    was always at the base of education
    as it was done,
so that education itself
    could be considered aberrative.

The Power of Simplicity Lectures

*Education
      can only become burdensome
when one is unable to not-know it.*

Scientology: The Fundamentals of Thought

*An evolution toward complexity
is an evolution
toward authoritarianism
and pomposity—
"You couldn't possibly understand this,
therefore I,
who pretend to,
am important"
is the attitude which mires learning.*

Handbook for Preclears

So long as a natural phenomenon
remains the knowledge of a few
and is denied to the many
it can be utilized to control the many.

Article: "The Loophole in Guarded Rights"

Authoritarians
do not achieve any results
beyond their own satisfaction—
which is not reason enough
for the student or technician
who wishes to get things done.

Handbook for Preclears

People are always attempting
to do more complicated things
and consider this good.
This isn't.
What people are doing, actually,
is losing their ability
to do simple things.

The Power of Simplicity Lectures

Authority belongs to those who can do the task in any given field.

Article: "Scientology's Future"

*The control and discipline
of imagination and its employment
for the artistic and practical gains
of the individual
would be the highest goal
of a training process.*

Article: "Child Scientology"

The only advice
I can give to the student
is to study a subject for itself
and use it exactly as stated,
then form his own opinions.
Study it with the purpose in mind
of arriving at his own conclusions
as to whether or not
the tenets he has assimilated
are correct and workable.
Compare what you have learned
with the known universe.

Seek for the reasons
    behind a manifestation,
and postulate the manner
    and in which direction
        the manifestation will likely proceed.
Do not allow the authority
    of any one person or school of thought
        to create a foregone conclusion
            within your sphere of knowledge.
Only with these principles
    of education in mind
        can you become
            a truly educated individual.

A New Slant on Life

On Imagination

$\mathcal{A}$n individual is as alive
as he has ideas.
He's as aware
as he has ideas.

Universes and the War Between Theta and MEST Lectures

*The basic definition of sanity
in this somewhat
nebulously learned society
is whether or not
a person agrees with everyone else.
It is a very sloppy manner
of accepting evidence,
but all too often
it is the primary measuring stick.*

Article: "How to Study Scientology"

A man is as well off
as his goals and dreams are intact.

Universes and the War Between Theta and MEST Lectures

One's appreciation of the MEST universe
is almost uniformly the energy
which one himself
places upon the MEST universe,
in other words his illusions.
When he loses his hopes and dreams
(his illusions),
it is because he has lost
his ability to emanate energy
back at the MEST universe
and is dependent upon the energy
the MEST universe thrusts at him.

Scientology 8-8008

If you want to get real tragic,
forget it was just magic.

The Route to Infinity Lectures: Appendix, "Dianetics Jingles"

People seek happiness in various ways,
hectically,
seriously,
desperately;
but the odd part of it is
that they find only
what they themselves put there.

Article: "Is It Possible to Be Happy?"

*I*magination
has a very superior value in thinking.
Any computation requires
that we imagine a situation
so that we can then resolve it.
If we cannot imagine eventualities,
we cannot prevent future failures.
One's ability to imagine
is directly proportional to
one's ability to be successful.

Self Analysis in Scientology

*Inaction and indecision in the present
is because of fear
of consequences
of the future.*

Technical Bulletin: "Future Processing"

The entire process
of thought
is an effort
to observe
something
without looking at it.

Technical Bulletin: "What the Thetan Is Trying to Do"

Delusion is imagination out of control.

Article: "Child Scientology"

*Imagination is all right
so long as you know it is imagination.
It is only
when one confuses it
with reality
that one gets into trouble.*

Self Analysis in Scientology

*Creative and constructive imaginings
about the future
are not untruths
but are postulated new realities.*

Science of Survival

Imagination is vital to computation, for it recombines for the purposes of creation, construction and prediction.

Article: "Dianometry, Your Ability and State of Mind"

What you've got to teach
a man to learn,
if you are going to teach him
to learn anything,
is you've got to teach him
to face his own illusions.

The Route to Infinity Lectures

Creative imagination
can be such a complex computation
and can be accomplished
on such thin data
by a good mind
that it can assume
an aspect of divine inspiration.

Article: "Dianometry, Your Ability and State of Mind"

*I*f a man can dream,
  if a man can have goals,
he can be happy and he can be alive.
  If he has no goals
  he doesn't even have a future.

Universes and the War Between Theta and MEST Lectures

On Thought

*Thought is the phenomenon
of combining,
imagining
or postulating
theta facsimiles
for the estimation
of future physical efforts.*

Advanced Procedure and Axioms

Thought
could be said to be
the resolution of maybes.

The Route to Infinity Lectures

Thought
consists entirely
of knowing and not-knowing
and the shades of gray between.

Scientology: The Fundamentals of Thought

*Computation is taking the maybes
out of existence.
So long as you can remove maybes
by the process of comparing data
and get a situation
which balances out yes or no,
you are thinking smoothly.*

The Route to Infinity Lectures

*The difference
between thought and matter
is that thought aligns
in its highest echelon,
and matter is chaos.*

The Philadelphia Doctorate Course Lectures

*The less certain
    the individual on any subject,
        the less sane he could be said
    to be upon that subject;
        the less certain he is
of what he views in the material universe,
    what he views in his own
            or the other fellow's universe,
    the less sane he could be said to be.*

A New Slant on Life

*Confusion is uncertainty.
Confusion is stupidity.
Confusion is insecurity.
When you think of uncertainty,
stupidity and insecurity,
think of confusion
and you'll have it down pat.*

The Problems of Work

It takes unknowingness,
joined to a game condition,
to bring about aberration.

The Power of Simplicity Lectures

An uncertainty
    is the product of two certainties.
        One of these is a conviction,
whether arrived at
        by observation (causative)
    or by a blow (effected).
        The other is a negative certainty.

A New Slant on Life

*P*rejudice:
   A fixed, unqualified opinion,
usually based on unhappy experience,
   substituting itself for reason.

Technical Bulletin: "Prejudice"

An unknown must be preceded
by a dependency to be aberrative.
A person was dependent on something,
and now he doesn't know
that he's still depending on it,
and he doesn't know
that it's still there.

The Power of Simplicity Lectures

*Looking into the past
and looking into the extreme future, alike,
are efforts to avoid present time
and efforts to look elsewhere
than at something.*

A New Slant on Life

Worry is constant,
irresolute computation
  — constant computation
on a certain point
  or a certain problem.

The Route to Infinity Lectures

$\mathcal{T}$he ability to think
is the capability of the mind
to perceive, pose and resolve
specific and general problems.

Article: "Dianometry, Your Ability and State of Mind"

*The lowest level of reasoning
is complete inability to differentiate,
which is to say,
identification.*

Science of Survival

*The highest level of reasoning
is complete differentiation.*

Science of Survival

Your enthusiasm
and zest for existence
comes mainly
from your ability to differentiate.

The Philadelphia Doctorate Course Lectures

Thinking
is not particularly hard to learn.
It consists merely
of comparing a particular datum
with the physical universe
as it is known and observed.

A New Slant on Life

*Every calculation of effort
made by the mind
is directed toward future.*

*The individual compares
conditions in the past
to observations in the present
in order to calculate efforts in the future.*

Advanced Procedure and Axioms

*Logic is the gradient scale
of relating facts
one to another.*

Scientology 8-8008

*A fact is something
that can be proven
to exist by visible evidence.*

Management Series: "The Anatomy of Thought"

81

*Association
is the essence of logic.*

Scientology 8-8008

Logic concerns obtaining answers.
And answers depend on **data**.
Unless you can test
and establish the truth
and value of the data being used,
one cannot attain right answers
no matter what Aristotle
may have said
or what IBM may have built.

Management Series: "Breakthroughs"

As you go way up Tone Scale,
you get less and less and less maybes,
        and you actually do less and less
and less computing,
        and you do more and more
                and more knowing.

The Route to Infinity Lectures

On Universes

A universe is simply
a point to view from,
plus the space and objects
which are put up there to view.

Universes and the War Between Theta and MEST Lectures

The universes, then,
are three in number:
the universe created by
one viewpoint,
the universe created by
every other viewpoint,
the universe created by
the mutual action of viewpoints
which is agreed to be upheld—
the physical universe.

Scientology 8-8008

*Universes are created
by the application of self-determinism
on eight dynamics.*

The Perception of Truth Lectures

*O*ne's own universe
　　is what he would construct
　　for a universe
without the opposition or the confusion
　　of other viewpoints.
　　The MEST universe
　　is that upon which one agrees
　　in order to continue in association
　　with other viewpoints.

Scientology 8-8008

The MEST *universe,*
according to any computation
one cares to make upon it,
is found to consist of
a high-level agreement amongst us.
Those who disagree
with the MEST *universe*
are punished by the MEST *universe.*

Scientology 8-8008

*T*he MEST universe seeks to own one
by pretending that immortality
is something difficult to buy
and is only purchased
by achieving an identity
or being an object.

Scientology 8-8008

*The postulate
of a god of a universe
is effective in that universe.
Corollary:
A universe is affected only
by the postulates
of the god of that universe.*

Universes and the War Between Theta and MEST Lectures

*I*t could be said, then,
that the difference between
the microcosm
(one's own universe)
and the macrocosm
(the MEST universe)
is the difference between
commanding it
and agreeing about it.

Scientology 8-8008

The first postulate
one would have to make
to make a universe
would be "I don't know."

The next postulate
he'd have to make
would be "There is something out there,"
and the next postulate
he'd have to make
would be "What is it?"

Universes and the War Between Theta and MEST Lectures

*M*otto of the
MEST Universe.
Thou Shalt Have No Force
Nor Illusion Nor Thine Own
Placement or Knowingness
in Space and Time
for All Illusion
Is Mine and
If Thou Art
I Shall Not
Be.

LRH Research Notes

*Despite its ferocity,
the universe is at best an illusion,
if a very solid one.
And the only thing
which can defeat it
is illusion.
When one loses the illusion of one's dreams,
when one no longer garbs
one's none-too-brilliant history
and rather perishable body with illusion,
life, bluntly and brutally,
isn't worth living.*

Self Analysis in Scientology

*This universe is organized
to immobilize a thetan.*

The Creation of Human Ability

*From the standpoint
of the MEST universe,
the greatest reality
would be had by matter itself
and this seems to be its evident goal
toward the thetan,
to make him into solid energy.*

Scientology 8-8008

*Self-determinism, applied,
will create,
conserve,
alter and possibly destroy
universes.*

The Perception of Truth Lectures

*If tone is to soar,
create even more.*

The Route to Infinity Lectures:
Appendix, "Dianetics Jingles"

One's universe
is an unthwarted sway,
the MEST universe is a compromise.

Scientology 8-8008

On
the Thetan

Once upon a time
there was a little thetan.
And he was a happy little thetan
and the world was a simple thing.
It was all very, very simple.
And then one day
somebody told him he was simple.
And ever since that time
he's been trying to prove
that he is not.

The Power of Simplicity Lectures

*Life is a static
which yet has the power
of controlling, animating,
mobilizing, organizing
and destroying
matter, energy and space
and possibly even time.*

Handbook for Preclears

*Freedom cannot be erased.
A static cannot be as-ised.*

The Creation of Human Ability

One of the control mechanisms
which has been used on thetans
is that when they rise in potential
they are led to believe themselves
one with the universe.
This is distinctly untrue.
Thetans are individuals.
They do not,
as they rise up the scale,
merge with other individualities.

They have the power
of becoming anything they wish
while still retaining
their own individuality.
They are first and foremost
themselves.

Scientology 8-8008

A static has no motion;
it has no width,
length,
breadth,
depth;
it is not held in suspension
by an equilibrium of forces;
it does not have mass;
it does not contain wavelengths;
it has no situation in time
or space.

Scientology 8-8008

Life is a unit energy source.
That energy source *is* the person,
the personality,
the center of beingness.

Self Analysis in Scientology

Man thought he had a human spirit.
That is totally incorrect.
Man is a human spirit
which is enwrapped more or less
in a mind
which is in a body.

Have You Lived Before This Life?

The thetan is immortal
and is possessed of capabilities
well in excess of those
hitherto predicted for man.

Scientology 8-8008

*Survival is a condition
susceptible to nonsurvival.
If one is "surviving,"
one is at the same moment
admitting that one can cease to survive,
otherwise one would never
strive to survive.
An immortal being
striving to survive
presents immediately a paradox.*

Scientology 8-8008

A thetan is indestructible.

The Creation of Human Ability

*The power
(defined as light-year kilotons
per microsecond)
of a thetan
is measured by nothing else
than the distance
(defined as spherical spatial length)
around him in his environment
that he can control.*

Technical Bulletin: "OT Maxims"

*Nothing can ever be done
directly to a thetan.
So the trick is,
one has to attach him to a possession,
and then hurt the possession.*

The Power of Simplicity Lectures

A thetan is understanding.
A space or mass is no understanding.
A thetan is no mass.
An object is mass.
Duplication is thus difficult.

The Creation of Human Ability

A thetan is the person himself—
not his body or his name,
the physical universe, his mind,
or anything else;
that which is aware of being aware;
the identity which is the individual.
The thetan is most familiar
to one and all as **you**.

Article: "Dianetics: Its Relationship to Scientology"

*The capabilities of the static
are not limited.*

Scientology 8-8008

*W*hen a thetan
exerts this power uncleverly,
he brings about destruction.

Technical Bulletin: "OT Maxims"

$\mathcal{Y}$our integrity to yourself
is more important than your body.

The Creation of Human Ability

The cold, basic truth
is that you are a vital
and necessary part of this world
and anything that is wrong with you,
you have assumed in an effort to be
what has passed for "human."

Handbook for Preclears

On Theta and MEST

*The goal of life
in the finite universe
may be easily and generally
defined as an effort to survive
as long as possible
and attain the most desirable
state possible
in that survival and,
in accomplishing this,
to conquer the physical universe.*

Handbook for Preclears

The cycle of existence for theta
consists of a disorganized
    and painful smash into MEST
    and then a withdrawal
    with a knowledge
        of some of the laws of MEST,
        to come back
        and smash into MEST again.

Science of Survival

The way out of MEST ain't detest.

The Route to Infinity Lectures: Appendix, "Dianetics Jingles"

Theta can become a problem
by its considerations,
but then becomes MEST.

The Creation of Human Ability

Mest could be considered
to be under onslaught by theta.
Theta could be considered to have
as one of its missions,
and its only mission
where MEST is concerned,
the conquest of the physical universe.
MEST is under raid.
Theta is doing the raiding.

Science of Survival

*Life is a game
wherein theta as the static
solves the problems of theta as MEST.*

The Creation of Human Ability

Capability is theta.

The Philadelphia Doctorate Course Lectures

Man alone
of the animal and vegetable kingdom
possesses the potential power
of changing MEST
in wholesale lots
into something theta can use.
Man can,
by steam shovel and dynamite,
move mountains and perhaps—
who knows?—conquer a galaxy.

Science of Survival

The purer the theta,
the more MEST will be attracted under it.

Science of Survival

*Theta crushed too hard
into MEST
becomes entheta.*

Science of Survival

*Entheta is just matter
kicking up a final splatter.*

The Route to Infinity Lectures:
Appendix, "Dianetics Jingles"

*It is an aspect of theta
that the more it is enturbulated
the easier it is
to enter enturbulence into it.*

Science of Survival

*One is as alive
as he has space
and as he can alter
and occupy that space.*

Scientology 8-8008

Space is a viewpoint of dimension.
Given a viewpoint and four,
eight or more points to view,
one has space.
Space is a problem of observation,
not of physics.

The Creation of Human Ability

Space, then,
is not an arbitrary and absolute
but it is creatable
or uncreatable by a viewpoint.

Scientology 8-8008

*Time is created,
at least in this universe,
by creating energy and objects,
and by being able to make
the universe agree with oneself,
not by having the universe
continually making one agree with it.*

Scientology 8-8008

*Time persists
because it is a lie deriving its force
from the absence of time
in the static.*

The Creation of Human Ability

*There is no space or time
beyond the space or time
necessary to hold the energy
which you create.*

Secrets of the MEST Universe Lectures

*The real way
to be assured of a great deal of time
is to be able, of course,
to create time,
and this would be to a thetan
the true concept of always.*

Scientology 8-8008

On
Aesthetics

*B*eauty is theta.

Scientology 8-80

*I*f beauty you desire,
beauty transpire.

The Route to Infinity Lectures: Appendix, "Dianetics Jingles"

Theta favors an aesthetic band because that's closest in to motionlessness; it's closest in to the fine wavelength which can append to theta itself.

The Philadelphia Doctorate Course Lectures

Any field which has critics galore,
wherein a thousand different schools
of divergent opinion can exist,
where opinion is listened to
with open mouths in lieu of reason
by which any man can reach a conclusion,
is an authoritarian field.
Aesthetics, unfortunately,
abounds in these critics and opinions.

Science of Survival

*Reason, analytical waves,
are too coarse to attain theta's zero
or infinity "wavelength."
Art alone may do so.*

Scientology 8-80

The first state above man
is a being who can communicate.
We instinctively revere the great artist,
painter or musician
and society as a whole looks upon them
as not quite ordinary beings.
And they are not.
They are a cut above Man.

Article: "Communication"

When a work of painting,
music or other form
attains two-way communication,
it is truly art.

Technical Bulletin: "Art and Communication"

All life is a repeating pulse and ebb and
surge of motion.

Life becomes difficult
when rhythmic prediction cannot occur.
Anxiety sets in.
It is a relief to participate
in predictable rhythm in an art form.
It is safe and reassuring.
If the rhythm is exciting
it is also exciting.
Therefore participation
in predictable rhythm
is pleasure and even joy.

Technical Bulletin: "Rhythm"

Art is the result of integration of all its components. One can add that the result invites contribution of and from the beholder.

Technical Bulletin: "Art and Integration"

*Compare, for example,
Rembrandt and the dilettante.
The dilettante does not know
how to paint, so most of his energy
goes into selecting the "right" brush
or the "apt" line or the "perfect" pigment.
Rembrandt does know how to paint.*

He picks up the first brush
that comes to hand,
  touches it to the palette and—wham!
A color. Rembrandt can be an artist,
  because he has a lot of technique
with which to be an artist.
  The dilettante has no technique,
and so he only plays the role of the artist.

Article: "Auditor First Should Know Tools Before He Goes in for Artistic"

*After an artist finishes
a piece of work,
    whether it is a story or anything else,
he should mock up the audience
    reading him.
This is really his most solid guarantee
    of any appreciation.*

Technical Bulletin: "Processing Notes"

*Doing things for self-satisfaction
is for professors who can't.*

Technical Bulletin: "Art Series 9"

*A professional knows the rules
of the game as a matter of course
so that he can achieve,
in the upper strata above that,
a high quality of art.*

Technical Bulletin: "A Professional"

W hat wave
        most closely approximates theta?
        It would be one
                of nearly infinite smallness,
        and that wave is found to be aesthetic,
the wavelength of the arts.

Scientology 8-80

*A*nd the opinion of the viewpoint
regulates the consideration of the forms,
their stillness or their motion,
and these considerations
consist of assignment of beauty
or ugliness to the forms
and these considerations alone are art.

Article: "This is Scientology, The Science of Certainty"

On Beingness

Decision:
The basic decision that life makes,
that theta makes,
is "to be or not to be."

The Route to Infinity Lectures

Article: "This is Scientology, The Science of Certainty"

The condition of being
is defined as the assumption
of a category of identity.
It could be said to be the role in a game
and an example of beingness
could be one's own name.
Another example would be
one's profession.
Another example would be
one's physical characteristics.
Each or all of these things
could be called one's **beingness.**

Scientology: The Fundamentals of Thought

The reason behind beingness is the drama of cause and effect.

Technical Bulletin: "Beingness and Certainty Processing"

*Any being is a viewpoint;
he is as much a being
as he is able to assume viewpoints.*

Scientology 8-8008

*That man who can be a great man
and at the same time
assume every other viewpoint there is,
is really a great man.*

Universes and the War Between Theta and MEST Lectures

The ideal group member is capable
of working causatively
in full cooperation with his fellows
in the achievement of group goals
and the realization
of his own happiness.

Technical Bulletin: "Robotism"

$\mathcal{A}$ professional is somebody
who can produce
a high-quality product.

Technical Bulletin: "A Professional"

Force yourself to smile
 and you'll soon stop frowning.

Force yourself to laugh
 and you'll soon find
  something to laugh about.

Wax enthusiastic
 and you'll very soon feel so.

A being causes
his own feelings.

The greatest joy there is in life
is creating.

Splurge on it!

Technical Bulletin: "The Joy of Creating"

*The discipline of beingness
is not necessarily
the limitation of beingness.
It is better to be able to decide
and control a few things to be,
than to be under the whip
of an imagination which drives one
to be a great many things,
none of which are under one's control.*

Article: "Child Scientology"

People don't *have* to be aberrated.

Organization Executive Course: "Good Workers"

Dramatizing is an apology for failure.

Advanced Procedure and Axioms

A thetan can be
what he can see.

Scientology 8-8008

*The limitation,
rather than the increase, of beingness
is the common course of existence.
One finds out "by experience"
(most of it incorrect)
that he cannot be a great many things.
His ability to be
is also his ability to communicate,
for the things which he is
are those things
which demark the amount of space
which he can occupy.*

Article: "Child Scientology"

*There is no trick to being
unless you spend your time agreeing.*

The Route to Infinity Lectures: Appendix, "Dianetics Jingles"

$\mathcal{D}$on't desire to be liked or admired.

The Creation of Human Ability

The more fixed
    the identity of the person may be,
    the less the experience
        of which he is capable.
Fame has at its end
    a completely fixed identification
        which is timeless,
but which unfortunately is matter
    and which equally unfortunately,
        is inaction.

Scientology 8-8008

*A man
who would have great understanding
would have also a brotherhood
with the entire universe.
He would also have
such nebulous qualities as charity.
Why?
Because he has a tolerance of viewpoints.*

Universes and the War Between Theta and Mest Lectures

On ARC

Theta,
the energy of thought and life,
has as primary manifestations
affinity,
reality
and
communication.

Science of Survival

$\mathcal{A}$ffinity
is a type
of energy
and can be produced
at will.

Scientology 8-8008

*The triangle
of affinity,
reality
and communication
could be called
an interactive triangle
in that no point of it can be raised
without affecting
the other two points
and raising them,
and no point of it
can be lowered
without affecting the other two points.*

The postulated reason
for this is that
affinity,
    reality
        and communication
are component parts of theta,
    and thus affinity,
reality and communication
    are three manifestations
    of the same thing.

Science of Survival

*People monitor their existence
by affinity.
Livingness is best expressed
in terms of affinity.*

The Power of Simplicity Lectures

$\mathcal{N}$ever permit
your affinity
to be alloyed.

The Creation of Human Ability

*Reality is agreement.
Too much agreement under duress
brings about the vanishment
of one's entire consciousness.*

Scientology 8-8008

Never compromise with your own reality.

The Creation of Human Ability

*Communication is far more important
than affinity or reality,
for it is the operation, the **action**,
by which one experiences emotion
and by which one agrees.
Communication is not only
the modus operandi,
it is the heart of life
and **is** by thousands of percent
the senior in importance
to affinity and reality.*

Scientology 8-8008

*The search for freedom
is either the retreat from
past failures to communicate
or the effort to attain new
communication.
To that degree then,
the search for freedom
is a sick or well impulse.*

Technical Bulletin: "Art"

$\mathcal{Y}$ou can say what you please
but what you say does not have to please.

Just be careful
  not too many people get unpleased.

Technical Bulletin: "Freedom of Speech"

Via is the curse word of existence.
Via means a relay point
in a communication line.
To talk *via* a body,
to get energy *via* eating alike
are communication byroutes.

The Creation of Human Ability

*Anything with which
you can fully communicate
cannot trouble you.*

The Power of Simplicity Lectures

$\mathcal{D}$o not give or receive
communication
unless you yourself desire it.

The Creation of Human Ability

Understanding is conceptual.
You could handle things,
objects and symbols endlessly
without achieving understanding
or real communication
unless one finally was able to
graduate up to conceptual comprehension.

Technical Bulletin: "Conceptual Understanding"

*Understanding
is composed of
affinity,
reality
and
communication.*

The Creation of Human Ability

*If you truly understand,
then you will be truly free.*

Universes and the War Between Theta and MEST Lectures

*The static has the capability
of total knowingness.
Total knowingness
would consist of total ARC.*

The Creation of Human Ability

*In order to have
an understanding of yourself,
you must have good ARC with yourself.*

*It is not evil to like yourself
or love yourself.
It is very low toned
not to be fond of yourself.*

Handbook for Preclears

*A person who is sane
has a high ARC value.*

Management Series: "The Missing Ingredient"

*Theta acting upon MEST
with affinity,
communication and reality
takes on an aspect known
as reasoning or understanding.
All mathematics can be derived
from ARC acting upon MEST.*

Science of Survival

*Theta's greatest potentialities
happen to be the ability to agree,
which makes for groups;
the ability to have an affinity,
to love and appreciate,
and to feel sensation,
and that is affinity;
and the ability to communicate,
and that's communication.*

The Philadelphia Doctorate Course Lectures

On Marriage and Family

*A family is a group
with the common goal of
group survival and advancement.*

Child Dianetics

*It has been discovered that
there are three kinds of love
between woman and man:
the first is covered under the law
of affinity and is the affection
with which mankind holds mankind;
the second is sexual selection
and is a true magnetism between partners;
the third is compulsive "love"
dictated by nothing more reasonable
than aberration.*

Dianetics: The Modern Science of Mental Health

Jealousy
    comes about because
        of the insecurity
            of the jealous person
    and the jealousy may
or may not have foundation.
    This person is afraid of
        hidden communication lines
            and will do anything to try
                to uncover them.

Article: "Marital Scientology"

Article: "Marital Scientology"

*Save the child
and you save the nation.*

Article: "Child Scientology"

A little child derives
all of his pleasure in life
from the grace he puts upon life.
He goes out in the morning
and looks at the day.
And it is a very, very beautiful day.
He looks at the flowers
and they are very beautiful.
He waves a magic hand
and brings all manner of
interesting things into being
in the environment.

Article: "Is it Possible to Be Happy?"

The little child
is quite bent on causing effects
and getting things admired.
He is continually being evaluated
in terms of what is to be admired.

Article: "This is Scientology, The Science of Certainty"

Education is also done in the home. The level of that education is the level of the home.

Handbook for Preclears

Children
   in present time
      are very easy to look after,
   very easy to instruct and to live with.
Children out of present time,
   bent on revenge,
      fresh from a quarrelsome
         breakfast table
            in an antipathetic home
               form a noisy and rebellious group.

Article: "Child Scientology"

*The goal of most parents
is obedience.
Obedience is apathy.
Most **bad** children become good
the moment you let them up
the Tone Scale.*

Handbook for Preclears

*A child needs security.
Part of that security is understanding.
Part of it is a code of conduct
which is invariable.
What is against the law today
can't be ignored tomorrow.*

Child Dianetics

The more one corrects
and punishes the child,
the less the child is there,
since correction in essence
is "go back into the past
and pick up punishing data
to remind you that the future
is going to be unpleasant."

Article: "Child Scientology"

A child is full of affinity.
   Not only does he have affinity
for his father, mother, brothers and sisters
and his playmates but for his dogs,
his cats and stray dogs
   that happen to come around.

Technical Bulletin: "The Theory of Affinity, Reality and Communication"

*Dignity and purpose
are native to the child;
badness and uncontrol are not.*

Article: "Child Scientology"

*Even beyond the fathering
and bearing
    and rearing of children,
a human being does not seem
    to be complete
    without a relationship
with a member of the opposite sex.*

This relationship is the vessel
wherein is nurtured
the life force
of both individuals,
whereby they create
the future of the race
in body and thought.

Science of Survival

On Human Society

$\mathcal{L}$iving
is a third-dynamic activity
for the most part.
And a person ceases to live
to the degree that he falls out of
this third dynamic.

The Power of Simplicity Lectures

*The primary human failing
is an inability to function as himself or
contribute to group achievements.*

Technical Bulletin: "Robotism"

When we have a society
which is very good at starting
we have a creative society.
When we have a society
which is very good at
keeping things running
we have a society that endures.
When we have a society
that is only capable of stopping things
we have a society which is destructive
or which is itself destroyed.

The Problems of Work

As slavery increases
in a country,
as freedom becomes less,
inflation and other economic evils
become more
because slave peoples
do not produce
and free peoples do.

Lecture: "Cause and Effect: Education, Unknowing Effect"

*Today we live in a vast cult
called "Worship the body."
Medical doctors, schoolteachers, parents,
traffic officers, the whole society
unites into this war cry,
"Care for the body."
This stems from the concept
that the body is all that one has,
that he will have just one body,
that his total devotion
is the care of that body.*

Article: "The Limitations of Homo Novis"

Man's wars,
his revolutions,
his suffering,
all stem from his lack of data
on the mind and man.

Article: "The Fight for Freedom"

*The artist injects
the theta into the culture,
and without that theta
the culture becomes reactive.*

Science of Survival

When the society at large
is having a very rough time
it contains a preponderance of individuals
who cannot help
and who cannot be helped.

Lecture: "Clear Procedure"

Help
is always betrayal
to a thoroughly aberrated person.

Technical Bulletin: "HELP"

*A government
wishing to deprave its people
to the point where they will accept
the most perfidious and rotten acts,
abolishes first the concept of God,
and in the wake of that
destroys the family, with "free love,"
the intellectual
with police-enforced idiocies,
and so reduces a whole population
to an estate somewhat below that of dogs.*

Science of Survival

No society
can exist
on a fabric of slaves.

All About Radiation

What element is necessary
in order to bring about slavery?
The element necessary is unwilling
and unknowing.
You could call those two elements
but they go hand in hand:
unknowing and unwilling
service to the state.

Lecture: "Cause and Effect: Education, Unknowing Effect"

Attempts at enslavement
arise primarily from fear.
Fear comes about with the loss of
confidence in one's ability
to make his way.
Thus is posed a world where
self-confidence is sought
by robbing others of theirs.
This cannot succeed
in a complex society.

Handbook for Preclears

*All great cathedrals began their building
by the placement of a single stone.
The building unit
of a great society
is the individual.*

Technical Bulletin: "Scientology Can Have a Group Win"

*I*t is interesting to note
that any society declines
in exact ratio to the contempt
in which it holds pleasure
and advances in ratio to the respect
it has for pleasure.

Science of Survival

*Human behavior
and human thought
are the foundation of human endeavor.*

Science of Survival

*A culture
is as rich and as capable of surviving
as it has imaginative artists,
skilled men of science,
a high ethic level,
workable government,
land and natural resources,
in about that order of importance.*

Science of Survival

*A basic knowledge of man
is essential to any improvement
in any area of the human race.*

Technical Bulletin: "Illiteracy and Work"

Never
desert a group to which
you owe your support.

The Creation of Human Ability

*Society,
thirsting for more control of more people
substitutes religion for the spirit,
the body for the soul,
an identity for the individual and
science and data for truth.
In this direction lies insanity,
increasing slavery, less knowingness,
greater scarcity and less society.*

The Creation of Human Ability

A society can only survive when it is built by the shoulders and hands of willing men.

All About Radiation

It is an empirical observation
that men without a strong
and lasting faith in a Supreme Being
are less capable, less ethical
and less valuable to themselves
and society.

Science of Survival

A group is as capable as it contains capable individual members.

Article: "What It Means to Be a Scientologist"

On
Force

Reason which is afraid of force
and reason which exists
to keep force from hurting one
is not reason.

The Philadelphia Doctorate Course Lectures

*This is a universe of force.
It is not a universe of reason.
Brutal, unthinking, without
decency or mercy, MEST force awaits
with punishment any being
with any weakness.*

Article: "The Limitations of Homo Novis"

*Man's ability
to handle destructive
physical universe forces
is far, far greater than his ability
to handle himself.*

Article: "The Goal of Training"

Man cannot be controlled
by force.
Man is controlled only
by his own willingness.

The Power of Simplicity Lectures

Man has a madness
and that madness is called war.

All About Radiation

As people descend the Tone Scale
they become more and more difficult
to communicate with
and things with which they will agree
become more and more solid.
Thus we have friendly discourse
high on the scale and war
at the bottom.
Where the affinity level is hate,
the agreement is solid matter,
and the communication . . . bullets.

Every bit of scientific lore
which has been accumulated
by scientists in the hope
that it may better
the lot of their fellow men
has eventually been employed
in the destruction of men.

All About Radiation

The history of war
is the history of control.
The end goal of war is
to throw out of its control
the population
of another government.

All About Radiation

$\mathcal{W}$ar:
Bad control
  having to be exerted
    because good control wasn't exerted.
      And this also defines destruction.

Technical Bulletin: "OT Maxims"

No revolution ever won anything.
Life evolves into a better condition
by means of hard work,
not by threats.

The Problems of Work

When cruelty
in the name of discipline
dominates a race,
that race has been taught to hate.
And that race
is doomed.

The real lesson is to learn to love.

A New Slant on Life

Evidently
war is not a good method
of controlling other nations
since it has never worked.
Man should observe from the errors
of the past that this method
never will work.

All About Radiation

*Any state which uses force
is doomed to failure.*

Notes on the Lectures of L. Ron Hubbard

Greatness
does not stem from savage wars
or being known.
It stems from being true
to one's own decency,
from going on helping others
whatever they do or think or say
and despite all savage acts against one;
to persevere without changing
one's basic attitude toward man.

A New Slant on Life

*It requires real strength
to love man.
And to love him despite
all invitations to do otherwise,
all provocations and all
reasons why one should not.*

A New Slant on Life

On Ethics and Justice

Ethics are reason.

Science of Survival

Man is basically good.
When he finds he is being
too destructive,
he recognizes he is bad for others
and seeks to leave.
He will also try to become less powerful,
ill or to kill himself.

Technical Bulletin: "Psychosis, More About"

*The highest ethic level
would be long-term survival concepts
with minimal destruction,
along any of the dynamics.*

Science of Survival

Some people cannot help.
They can only injure and destroy.
And if in the name of help
they only injure and destroy,
then know them carefully,
for they are criminals.

Technical Bulletin: "By Their Actions . . ."

*When an individual
is acting contrary to survival
of himself, his group, progeny,
race, mankind or life
he can be considered
to be unintelligent, uninformed
or aberrated.*

The Dynamics of Life

Ethics
actually consist of rationality
toward the highest level of survival
for the individual,
the future race,
the group and mankind,
and the other dynamics
taken collectively.

Science of Survival

<An optimum solution
   to any problem would be
that solution which brought
the greatest benefits
   to the greatest number of dynamics.

Scientology 8-8008

*Human beings
have a very high
native sense of justice.*

Advanced Procedure and Axioms

*A sin is misusing
a counter-effort you have received.*

The Route to Infinity Lectures

*I*n the matter of being right
or being wrong,
a lot of muddy thinking can develop.
There are no absolute rights
or absolute wrongs.
And being right does not consist
of being unwilling to harm,
and being wrong
does not consist
only of not harming.

A New Slant on Life

There is freedom
in knowing what is thought right,
what is thought wrong.
There is only slavery
when nobody knows
and the rules are all "off the cuff."

Organization Executive Course: "Justice"

*Agreement
to what ought to be
and then a shattering of the troth
works all the spell that's needed
for a recipe of misery.*

Technical Bulletin: "Clean Hands Make a Happy Life"

The least-free person
is the person who cannot reveal
his own acts and who protests
the revelation of the improper acts
of others.

A New Slant on Life

$\mathcal{A}$ man
with a clean heart
can't be hurt.

Organization Executive Course: "Blow-Offs"

*The insane
are just one seething mass
of overt acts and withholds.
And they are very
physically sick people.*

Management Series: "Ethics"

*The man or woman
who must must must become a victim
and depart is departing
because of his or her
own overts and withholds.*

Organization Executive Course: "Blow-Offs"

The lowest confront there is
is the confront of evil.

Organization Executive Course:
"Conditions, How to Assign"

*An inability to confront evil
leads people into disregarding it
or discounting it or not seeing it at all.*

Management Series: "Ethics"

$\mathcal{J}$ustice could be called
the adjudication
of the relative rightness or wrongness
of a decision or an action.

Advanced Procedure and Axioms

*T*he idea of not harming anything
and helping everything
are alike rather mad.
It is doubtful if you would think
helping enslavers was a beneficial
action and equally doubtful
if you would consider
the destruction of a disease
an overt act.

A New Slant on Life

Article: "Fast Justice"

*One must act,
one must preserve
order and decency,
but one need not hate
or seek vengeance.*

A New Slant on Life

On Lies and Truth

Truth is the exact consideration.
Truth is the exact

time,
place,
form and
event.

The Creation of Human Ability

*Y*ou are truth.

Personal Achievement Series Lecture: "The Road to Truth"

*W*e can achieve a persistence
only when we mask a truth.

The Creation of Human Ability

*In a PR world,
truth is the almost unknown commodity.
This world is full
of the "noise" of many lies,
many babbles,
many old fixations and hates.*

Management Series: "The Missing Ingredient"

Stupidity is the unknownness
of consideration.

Mechanical definition:
Stupidity is the unknownness
of time, place,
form and
event.

The Creation of Human Ability

*False data,
lack of data
and misevaluated data
cause the errors of computation.*

Article: "Dianometry, Your Ability and State of Mind"

*The road to ruin
is paved with false information.*

Article: "False Reports"

*Lying is an alteration of
time,
place,
event or form.
Lying becomes alter-isness,
becomes stupidity.*

The Creation of Human Ability

Man is not happy
unless he is honest.
White, black, red or brown,
this is true of all times and all races.

Technical Bulletin: *"Students Who Succeed"*

Truth has comm value.
All the lies will dead-end someday.

Management Series: "The Missing Ingredient"

*There is an ethic
about the handling of truth.
While it may be true that
something is undesirable or that
a person is bad,
if it serves no good purpose
to make the statement,
the issuance of this "truth"
is in reality the establishing
of an entheta line.*

Science of Survival

*Anything which has wide acceptance
and has been successful,
wherever suns shine
and planets swing,
is based upon some fundamental truth.*

Scientology 8-8008

*Absolutes
are unobtainable.*

The Philadelphia Doctorate Course Lectures

*T*here are two ways
men ordinarily accept things,
neither of them very good.
One is to accept a statement
because Authority says it is true
and must be accepted,
and the other is by preponderance
of agreement amongst other people.

Article: "How to Study Scientology"

*The highest one can attain to truth
is to attain to his own illusions.*

Scientology 8-8008

*The old must give way
to the new,
falsehood must become exposed by truth,
and truth,
though fought,
always in the end prevails.*

Article: "My Philosophy"

On the
Nature of
Man

*Actual experience
demonstrates that man,
once socially imposed controls
and domination by others
have been cleared away,
is basically good.
He is evil only when he is aberrated.*

Science of Survival

Man is not a machine,
however much he loves machinery.
Whatever man consists of,
he is basically not evil.
He is merely ignorant.

All About Radiation

*H*uman beings,
    operating along all the dynamics,
      are actually rather heroic
      and noble characters.
  They see cruelty or suffering and they,
    particularly in their youth
      and strength,
  take it on to spare the world.
      They see someone,
      even themselves,
      perform a cruel act
  or have an unhappy experience,
    and they regret it.

*Then they discover
    that they themselves can fail.
They then blame others
    for their plight.
It is a cycle of nobly accepting something
    and then,
        to save one's own being,
trying to get rid of it in time.*

Handbook for Preclears

A man
without an abiding faith is,
by observation alone,
more of a thing than a man.

Science of Survival

It is a demonstrable law,
not an opinion,
that he who would enslave his fellows
becomes himself enslaved.

Handbook for Preclears

Men are rather thoroughly stuck
in the present
and so involved with its confusions
that they rarely foresee anything
and are mainly oblivious
to any consequences
of their own actions
or failures to act.

This gives them the appearance
of being stupid.

Technical Bulletin: "Prediction and Consequences"

*You can't have a civilization
without able citizens.
It is impossible
to have a working democracy
without its ranks including
only intelligent and capable individuals.
Five morons
do not make a genius.*

LRH Note: "Ability Book"

*The human mind
is capable of resolving
the problem of the human mind.*

A New Slant on Life

*The individual himself
is a spirit controlling a body
via a mind.*

Scientology: The Fundamentals of Thought

The senior entity is the thetan,
for without the thetan
there would be no mind
or animation in the body,
while without a body or a mind
there is still animation and life
in the thetan.

Scientology: The Fundamentals of Thought

The physical body was built
in the time when escapes from death
    by wild animals,
    by falling, were routine.
It was built in an operating climate
    of great hazard over a period
    of many millions of years.
It requires about three escapes
    from sudden death daily
    to stay in present time.

The Creation of Human Ability

Silly Optimist:
A person who expects to feel well
all the time
while running a meat body.

Technical Bulletin: "Temperatures"

*Cause is the life static itself.
Full effect would be MEST,
or a dead body.*

Advanced Procedure and Axioms

*I*n seeking to survive,
a person still possessed of some vigor
will seek to be and always asserts
that he is right.

Article: " 'Being Cause' is Society's Major Aberration"

$\mathcal{B}$eings on the way down
don't believe they are wrong
  because they don't dare believe it.
And so they do not change.

A New Slant on Life

Probably you could kill a man with sympathy. It has been done.

Handbook for Preclears

*A fully reasonable human being
displays the emotion called for,
rationally,
by the circumstances with which
he is confronted in present time.*

Science of Survival

A high-tone individual
thinks wholly into the future.
He is extroverted toward his environment.
He clearly observes the environment
with full perception
unclouded by undistinguished fears
about the environment.
He thinks very little about himself
but operates automatically
in his own interests.

He enjoys existence.
His calculations
(postulations and evaluations)
are swift and accurate.
He is very self-confident.
He knows he knows
and does not even bother to assert
that he knows.
He controls his environment.

Advanced Procedure and Axioms

*S*ingle men
and determined groups
have been the only makers of space
in which man could walk free.

Technical Bulletin: "Purpose"

Man can save his soul.
Like the bright cool dawn
after a night of prison and of thunder,
man can taste
that freedom sought so long.

Article: "An Invitation to Freedom, Man *Can* Save His Soul"

There are those who would tell you
        that only a fiend would set you free,
and that freedom leads at best
into the darkest hells,
        and there are those to inform you
                that freedom is for you
                        and not for them,

but there are also
    men of kind heart
who know how precious is the cup
and drink of wide,
        unbounded ways.

The Creation of Human Ability

On
Self-Determinism

The common denominator
of all life impulses
is self-determinism.

The Perception of Truth Lectures

The essence of a man
is his self-determinism.

Self Analysis in Scientology

Self-determinism may be defined
as the location of matter and energy
in space and time,
as well as a creation of time and space
in which to locate matter and energy.

The Perception of Truth Lectures

*Choice is the keynote
of self-determinism.
To determine anything,
you must have the choice to determine.
Choice to determine
means that you must have
the power of decision.*

The Route to Infinity Lectures

Decision and time
have a lot in common.
When we have clean, clear decision,
we have clean, clear time.
And when we have an indecision,
there is an unclarity about time.

The Route to Infinity Lectures

Q and A

is the disease of dodging life.

Technical Bulletin: "The Cure of Q and A, Man's Deadliest Disease"

The reason an individual
cannot approach a future goal
or even strongly postulate one
lies in his inability
to resolve the present
or to make a decision in the past.

Advanced Procedure and Axioms

*Cause
is motivated by the future.*

Scientology 8-8008

*A man without future goals
is a worried and sick man.*

Advanced Procedure and Axioms

The deterioration of the individual is the deterioration of his own determinism.

Universes and the War Between Theta and Mest Lectures

Your self-determinism
and your honor
  are more important
than your immediate life.

The Creation of Human Ability

*I*t can be readily established
that an individual
loses his self-determinism
in the ratio that he possesses objects
and utilizes force.

Scientology 8-8008

We are all self-determined, natively. Nothing which we do is beyond self-determined action.

Handbook for Preclears

Postulates alone aberrate the individual.

Advanced Procedure and Axioms

*A postulate
is that self-determined thought
which starts, stops or changes
past, present or future efforts.*

Advanced Procedure and Axioms

*Individual postulates
are always senior
to any pattern of agreements.*

Universes and the War Between Theta and Mest Lectures

Q and A

is simply Postulate Aberration.

Technical Bulletin: "The Reason for Q and A"

On Play

The most valuable thing
that a thetan possesses
is his spirit of play.

The Philadelphia Doctorate Course Lectures

Agreement to rules and penalties
is necessary to continue a game.

The Philadelphia Doctorate Course Lectures

$\mathcal{T}$he highest ability
in playing a game
would be the ability
to know the rightness
and wrongness rules
of that particular game.

A New Slant on Life

$\mathcal{W}$hat's a good rule?
It is a rule which aligns action
and permits compliance.

The Philadelphia Doctorate Course Lectures

*One can have a game
and know it.
He can be in a game
and not know it.
The difference is his determinism.*

Dianetics 55!

Games require space
and havingness.
A game requires other players.

Games also require skill
and knowingness
that they are games.

Dianetics 55!

*You've got to have complexity
in a game; otherwise,
it becomes monotonous.*

The Philadelphia Doctorate Course Lectures

*Interest is mainly kindled
by the unpredictable.*

The Problems of Work

*Y*ou have to invent boredom
to get bored.

The Power of Simplicity Lectures

*I*f you want to last
just move fast.

The Route to Infinity Lectures: Appendix, "Dianetics Jingles"

When a game is done
    the player keeps around tokens.
These are hopes the game will start again.
When that hope is dead
    the token, the terminal, is hidden.
And it becomes an automaticity
    —a game going on below
        the level of knowingness.

Dianetics 55!

*I*nsanity
is an unknowing games condition.

The Power of Simplicity Lectures

*If a man
had all the attention in the world
he would be unhappy.
If he had all the identities possible,
he would still be unhappy.
If he could blow up Earth
or create any other huge effect
he wanted (without limit),
he would be miserable
(or as insane).
If he could own everything
everywhere
he would be dulled to apathy.*

Scientology: The Fundamentals of Thought

One loses to the degree
he is forbidden to have.
But to play a game
one must be able to believe
he can't have.

Scientology: The Fundamentals of Thought

The more serious you take the game,
the less chance there is
of winning.

The Philadelphia Doctorate Course Lectures

The prize of winning
is making a new game
or permitting a new game to be made
or making it possible
for a new game to be played.

The Philadelphia Doctorate Course Lectures

You can't stand
bowing back of the footlights forever
  with no show
even if you are quite an actor.

Somebody else can make better use
  of any stage
    than even the handsomest actor
    who will not use it.

*To win
one must wish to win;
when one no longer desires to win,
one no longer desires to live.*

Scientology 8-8008

On Courage

Courage

might be considered the theta force
necessary to overcome obstacles
in surviving.

Science of Survival

Many beings

live lives of quiet correctness
without ever once making anything
do anything.
Things around them just happen
to be orderly.
The social system props them up.

But someday—bang—the society
  gets into a turmoil
      which knocks out the props.
Then we see
    that there were too few present
        who could make things go right
            and that is the end of the society.
Thus died all old civilizations.

Organization Executive Course: "The Supreme Test"

*To solve any problem
it is only necessary
to become theta, the solver,
rather than theta, the problem.*

The Creation of Human Ability

When you start to introduce order
into anything,
    disorder shows up and blows off.
Therefore, efforts to bring order
    in the society or any part of it
will be productive of disorder
    for a short while every time.

A New Slant on Life

*Almost anyone,
no matter his position,
can remedy a situation
no matter what's wrong
if he or she really wants to.*

Organization Executive Course: "Blow-Offs"

*The persistency
of the individual in life
is directly governed
by the strength of his basic dynamic.*

The Dynamics of Life

You face force
    with reason
and continue to apply reason.
    A human being goes into apathy
when stopped from doing this.

Notes on the Lectures of L. Ron Hubbard

Strength is nothing
without skill and tech
and, reversely,
without skill and tech
the strength of brutes
is a matter of contempt.

Organization Executive Course: "Ethics, the Design Of"

Arrogance and force
may win dominion and control
but will never win
acceptance and respect.

Management Series: "Manners"

*Strength has two sides,
one for good and one for evil.
It is the intention
that makes the difference.*

Organization Executive Course: "Ethics, the Design Of"

The man who has no impulse
to set things right
is insane.

Personal Achievement Series Lecture:
"Operation Manual for the Mind"

Man is solving himself
to extinction.
And all on the slogan
"Don't exert yourself."

Organization Executive Course: "Artistic Presentation"

Courage could be summed up in
(1) being willing to cause something,
and
(2) going ahead to achieve the effect
one has postulated
against any and all odds.

The Philadelphia Doctorate Course Lectures

*The power of the individual
is his ability to
initiate the resolution of problems
and execute the solutions.*

Article: "Dianometry, Your Ability and State of Mind"

Luck is the hope
that some uncontrolled chance
will get one through.
Counting on luck
is an abandonment of control.
That's apathy.

The Problems of Work

*If you reduce a man's effort
output to zero
you will also collapse his bank
on him.*

Organization Executive Course: "Artistic Presentation"

Efficiency could be defined
as the ability to play the game to hand.
Inefficiency could be defined
as an inability to play the game to hand,
with a necessity to invent games
with things
which one should actually be able
to control with ease.

The Problems of Work

*There is an area of existence
known as experience —
the willingness to experience.
And when an individual
will not have anything further to do
with something,
he becomes the effect of it.*

Lecture: "Dianetics 1961 and the Whole Solution
to the Problems of the Human Mind"

*The entire source of pain
is an effort to abstain.*

The Route to Infinity Lectures:
Appendix, "Dianetics Jingles"

*The handling of a problem
seems to be simply
the increase of ability
to confront the problem,
and when the problem
can be totally confronted,
it no longer exists.
This is strange and miraculous.*

A New Slant on Life

On Work

*A post or job
is enormously valuable.
Even the most minor post
has a status value.*

Management Series: "Ethics and Personnel"

W

When a person has no hat
he lacks purpose and value.

Management Series: "Hats"

People live Q and A lives.
They never become
what they desire to be
because they Q-and-A
with life about it.

Schopenhauer,
the German philosopher of doom,
even had a dirty crack
about being able to do things:
"Stubbornness is the will
taking the place of the intellect."
By this, one is "intellectual"
if he Qs-and-As.

Technical Bulletin: "The Reason for Q and A"

If anything will kill Western society,
it is either
tremendous political blunders
which bring about an atomic war,
or
this philosophy that work
is too hard to confront.

All About Radiation

A common method
employed by low-toned people
to reduce the power and ability
of an individual
and so place him under control
is to convince him
that he is tired and overworked.
If they can so convince him,
they can then get him to take a vacation.

An examination of an individual
who has been subjected to this
will show that he was happiest
when he was working
and that before he "needed a vacation"
many people worked on him
to convince him
that he should not work so hard,
and thus turned
what was actually play to him
into work.

Scientology 8-8008

People have to be told
and kept in the frame of mind
that life is worth living
and that things are worth doing.

All About Radiation

Beware these people who come around
and inquire "sympathetically"
about your health
because you look "overworked."
It is almost easier to get "overloafed"
than overworked.

The Problems of Work

*I*t is only when something
makes man unwilling,
stops him too often
and kills his interest
in what he is doing
that he becomes exhausted.

All About Radiation

However you view it
or however it was done,
failure to provide
jobs,
purpose
and training on jobs
begets revolt.

Management Series: "Ethics and Personnel"

One can even trace
the unrest of a nation
to lack of purpose and value.
A huge welfare program
guarantees crime and revolt
because it gives handouts,
not hats.

Management Series: "Hats"

Where we have fault
to find with working,
it grows out of our own fear
that we will not be permitted
to continue work.

The Problems of Work

Great revolutions occur
out of a mass inability to work.
The crowds rebel
not because they are angry over privileges,
which they always say,
but because they have gone mad,
having no work.

The Problems of Work

If governments and civilizations
continue to produce things
to convince people that they are just slaves
and that things aren't worth doing
and that they have to be pushed
into work with a whip,
the whole society degenerates.

All About Radiation

*W*ork
is admission of inability to play.

The Philadelphia Doctorate Course Lectures

People who can't get things done
are simply Q-and-Aing
with people and life.
People who **can** get things done
just don't Q-and-A.

All great truths are simple.

This is a major one.

Technical Bulletin: "The Reason for Q and A"

*S*omebody invented the difference
between work and play.
Play was seen to be something
that was interesting
and work was seen to be something
that was arduous and necessary
and therefore not interesting.
But when we have our vacations
and go and "play" we are usually very glad
to get back to the "daily grind."
Play is almost purposeless.
Work has a purpose.

The Problems of Work

Society almost demands
that a man consider whatever he is doing
as work
and demands that he consider work
as an unhappy thing.

Scientology 8-8008

If all the workmen
in America and England
became unwilling to work,
one would again see a barbarism.

All About Radiation

Tiredness
is willingness gone bad.

All About Radiation

If you are afraid of losing your job,
it is because you suffer already
from too many forbiddings to work.
The only way to hold a job
is to make it every day,
to create it and keep it created.
If you have no wish to create
and continue that job
then there must be something
at cross-purposes with purpose.
There is something wrong between
what you think would be a good purpose
and what purpose your job has.

The Problems of Work

On Havingness

By havingness we mean
owning,
 possessing,
  being capable of commanding,
positioning,
 taking charge of objects,
  energies or spaces.

Scientology: The Fundamentals of Thought

In life experience matter becomes havingness.

Article: "SOP 8-C:
The Rehabilitation of the Human Spirit"

Havingness:
That which permits
the experience of mass and pressure.

The Creation of Human Ability

*To be nothing,
to disappear
or have its possessions disappear
is the main terror of the thetan
and is, indeed,
his only terror.*

Technical Bulletin:
"The Theta–MEST Theory Extended"

Loss itself can occur only
when the consideration that
one **wants, needs, has to have,**
has occurred first.

The Creation of Human Ability

*The sensation of pain
is actually a sensation of loss.
It is a loss of beingness,
a loss of position
and awareness.*

Article: "This is Scientology, The Science of Certainty"

The way a being is hung
   with persistent masses
      is the mechanism of getting him
   to believe certain things are undesirable.
These he cannot then have.
      He can only combat them
         or ignore them.
            Either way they are not as-ised.
            Thus, they persist.

Organization Executive Course: "Responsibility Again"

*To own
is to be able to see
or touch or occupy.*

Scientology: The Fundamentals of Thought

That which one cannot accept
he cannot as-is.

The Creation of Human Ability

The essential definition of *having*
is to be able to touch or permeate
or to direct the disposition of.

Scientology: The Fundamentals of Thought

*P*ersistence simply comes about
through an inability
to create or destroy something.

Universes and the War Between Theta
and Mest Lectures

*There are millions of methods
of possession in life.
    The obvious one becomes overlooked.
If one can see a thing
he can have it—if he thinks he can.*

Scientology: The Fundamentals of Thought

On Living

*There is no substitute for an all-out, over-the-ramparts, howling charge against life. That's **living**.*

The Route to Infinity Lectures

Knowing about life would also have to include knowing about death.

Article: "How Do People Know They Have Lived Before?"

If you are frightened
of losing your pocketbook,
if you are frightened
of losing your memory,
if you are frightened
of losing your girl or your boyfriend,
if you are frightened
of losing your body—well that is how
frightened you ought to be of dying,
because it is all the same order
of magnitude.

Have You Lived Before This Life?

A person with amnesia
is looked upon as ill.
What of a person
who can remember only this life?
Is this then
not a case of amnesia
on a grand scale?

Have You Lived Before This Life?

*Death is actually a gradient scale.
Small mishaps and accidents
can tend toward greater and greater
accumulation of mishaps and accidents,
until death of an ambition,
death of an individual,
death of a cause
or death of a group is attained.*

Science of Survival

*Run any equation
into which pain has entered
and it can be seen that it reduces down
to possible nonsurvival.
And if this were all there were
to surviving
and if necessity
were a vicious little gnome
with a pitchfork,
it seems rather obvious that there would
be scant reason to go on living.*

Dianetics: The Modern Science
of Mental Health

Life is not much worth living
if it cannot be enjoyed.

Science of Survival

$\mathcal{P}$leasure is the positive commodity.
It is enjoyment of work,
contemplation of deeds well done;
it is a good book or a good friend;
it is taking all the skin off one's knees
climbing the Matterhorn;
it is hearing the kid
first say "Daddy";
it is a brawl on the Bund at Shanghai
or the whistle of amour from
a doorway; it's adventure
and hope and enthusiasm
and "someday I'll learn to paint";

it's eating a good meal
or kissing a pretty girl
    or playing a stiff game of bluff
      on the stock exchange.
It's what man does
    that he enjoys doing;
      it's what man does
    that he enjoys contemplating;
    it's what man does
      that he enjoys remembering;
and it may be just the talk of things
he knows he'll never do.

*Dianetics: The Modern Science
of Mental Health*

$\mathcal{H}$appiness
is applied individual effort.

Advanced Procedure and Axioms

Happiness is important.
The ability to arrange life
and the environment
so that living can be better enjoyed,
the ability to tolerate
the foibles of one's fellow humans,
the ability to see
the true factors in a situation
and resolve problems of living
with accuracy,
the ability to accept
and execute responsibility,
these things are important.

Science of Survival

Never let it be said of you
that you lived an amateur life.

A New Slant on Life

If you have the idea
about **anything** you do
that you just dabble in it,
you will wind up with a dabble life.
There'll be no satisfaction in it
because there will be no real production
you can be proud of.

A New Slant on Life

An individual is evidently designed to be cause.

Advanced Procedure and Axioms

There is nothing to be gained by backing up from life. That isn't the way out, except through the bottom.

The Route to Infinity Lectures

If motion from you flows,
> the world glows.

The Route to Infinity Lectures:
Appendix, "Dianetics Jingles"

*Our attitude toward life
makes every possible difference
to our living.
It is not necessary
to study a thousand ancient books
to discover this fact;
but sometimes
it needs to be pointed out again.
Life does not change so much
as our attitude toward it.*

Article: "Is It Possible to Be Happy?"

L*ife is a series of attained goals.*

Technical Bulletin: "Goals in the Rudiments"

*Living does not consist
of sitting in a temple in the shadows
and getting rheumatism
from the cold stones.
Living is hot,
it's fast,
it's often brutal!*

The Route to Infinity Lectures

So long as an organism
can employ in its survival
a counter-effort,
that counter-effort is not aberrative.

Advanced Procedure and Axioms

*If there is any trouble
with the preclear,
it is that the environment
is insufficiently dangerous
and so does not produce
sufficient amusement.*

The Creation of Human Ability

On
Power

The totality of power
is orderly progress.

Organization Executive Course: "Justice"

Man can seldom handle power. He retreats from it or abuses it. When he has it he often misdirects it.

Article: "The States of Existence"

If one would live a life of command
 or one near to a command,
  one must then accumulate power
  as fast as possible
   and delegate it as quickly as feasible
 and use every humanoid in long reach
to the best and beyond his talents
if one is to live **at all.**

Management Series: "The Responsibilities of Leaders"

*The leader is that one
who emotionally affects others
most strongly toward positive action.*

Handbook for Preclears

Be your own adviser,
keep your own counsel
and select your own decisions.

The Creation of Human Ability

*Don't ever feel weaker
because you work for somebody stronger.
The only failure lies in taxing
or pulling down the strength
on which you depend.*

Management Series: "The Responsibilities of Leaders"

*When you let a person
give nothing for something,
you are factually encouraging crime.*

Management Series: "Ethics"

It is exchange
which maintains the inflow and outflow
that gives a person space around him
and keeps the bank off of him.

Management Series: "Ethics"

*A*bove case gain is competence.

Organization Executive Course: "Competence"

*W*hat is a great feat?
It's something
  that can't be duplicated.

The Power of Simplicity Lectures

*The whole feeling
of self-confidence and competence
actually derives from one's ability
to control or leave uncontrolled
the various items and people
in his surroundings.*

The Problems of Work

If you are afraid of people,
you won't trust yourself
and will be afraid
of what you might do.

Handbook for Preclears

*T*ry to give somebody
something he doesn't want
and you are going to overthrow
his power of choice.
His power of choice
is the only thing
that he had to begin with,
which gave him power,
capability and anything else
and that power of choice
has been consistently
and continuously overthrown

by giving him things he didn't want
and taking away from him
things he didn't want
to get rid of
back and forth.
You get the individual
pretty overwhelmed
and he goes down in power.

Technical Bulletin: "Recognition of Rightness of the Being"

People do not acquire obsessively
those things which they do not fear.
An individual has to resist something,
has to be afraid of something,
has to be afraid
of the consequences of something
before it can have any adverse
obsessive effect upon him.

Dianetics 55!

That which one cannot accept
chains one.

For instance, revulsion to sex inclines at last to slavery to sex. A ruler's motto could be "make them resist," and his people would become slaves. In 1870 we find capitalists resisting Marx. In 1933, we find Marx the basic text of US government. Resistance and restraint
are the barbed wire
of this concentration camp.
Accept the barbed wire
and there is no camp.

The Creation of Human Ability

*Never need praise,
approval or sympathy.*

The Creation of Human Ability

*When an individual
is totally for himself
and nobody else,
or when he is totally for everybody else
and not for himself,
he alike perishes.*

Personal Achievement Series Lecture:
"Power of Choice and Self-Determinism"

*If one assigns cause to something,
     he delivers to that entity power.*

Advanced Procedure and Axioms

*There are gods above all other gods,
and gods beyond the gods of universes,
     but it were better,
          far better,
     to be a raving madman in his cell
than to be a thing with the ego,
          cruelty and jealous lust
               that base religions have set up
     to make men grovel down.*

Scientology 8-8008

*I*njustice is not something in which
any man with power
should ever trade.
It is not just a sin.
It is suicide.

Technical Bulletin: "Riots"

When one speaks of responsibility he means "the determination of the cause which produced the effect."

Advanced Procedure and Axioms

Life is, or can be,
a pretty grim proposition.
        One may float along
                on the production of others
like the recently demised "leisure class"
                of 19th century infamy
        or like a hobo being chased
by every householder and cop.
One can go along in the numb world
        of the middle class
                watching his public docility
while he hypocritically sins behind doors
        and conforms with a capital C.

One can creakingly labor
in the world of the endlessly-
being-dug ditch
for some unknown pipe.
Or one can simply confront
the whole thing, pain, misemotion,
punishments, rewards and all
and produce and exchange
and learn to handle
the administrative system he is in
and himself administer
his life and environ.

Management Series: "Admin Know-How No. 30"

$\mathcal{P}$eople who get things done
are at cause.

Technical Bulletin: "The Cure of Q and A,
Man's Deadliest Disease"

*There are those
who talk about "lucky breaks"
and who speak of the "hand of fate"
in their undertakings,
but a forthright examination
of the field of man's activities
will show that nearly all success
is most adequately deserved.*

Science of Survival

On
Responsibility

*It is folly to try to control something
or even know something
without responsibility.*

Management Series: "The Top Triangle"

*Responsibility is the ability
and willingness
to assume the status
of full source and cause
for all efforts and counter-efforts
on all dynamics.*

Advanced Procedure and Axioms

*The keynote of responsibility
is the willingness to handle energy.*

Scientology 8-8008

*Good Control:
        Harmonious alignment.
Bad Control:
        Disharmonious alignment.*

Technical Bulletin: "OT Maxims"

We can define responsibility
as the concept of being able to care for,
to reach or to be.
To be responsible for something
one does not actually
have to care for it
or reach it or be it.
One only needs to believe or know
that he has the ability to care for it,
reach it or be it.

Organization Executive Course:
"Responsibility Again"

$\mathcal{F}$ull responsibility is not fault;
it is recognition of being cause.

Advanced Procedure and Axioms

A soldier shot on the field of battle
may "blame" the sniper,
Selective Service,
the stupidity of government,
but he nevertheless had full responsibility
not only for being there
and getting shot
but for the sniper,
Selective Service
and the stupidity of government.

Advanced Procedure and Axioms

*I*f you blame somebody hard enough
and long enough,
you have kept on electing them
as cause
until they are much more powerful
than yourself.

Handbook for Preclears

*One becomes that to which
he assigns responsibility
too often and too long.
He makes it **cause** and, at last,
to be cause himself,
he must be the thing.*

Scientology 8-80

One obtains randomity
by abandoning responsibility
in some sphere.
He will then find himself
in conflict in that sphere.

Scientology 8-8008

When good sense and
good judgment
   are not added into control,
control gets a bad name.

Technical Bulletin:
"OT Maxims"

All real difficulty stems from no responsibility.

Organization Executive Course: "Responsibility Again"

Aberration is a chain of vias based on a primary nonconfront.

Technical Bulletin: "Complexity and Confronting"

By responsibility is meant
the area or sphere of influence
the individual can rationally affect
around other people,
life, MEST,
and the general environment.

Science of Survival

One does not send to find
for whom the bell tolls
   without full willingness
      to have tolled it
and to have caused
      the cause of its tolling.

Advanced Procedure and Axioms

A being can of course
run away from life (blow)
and go sit on the backside of the moon
and do nothing and think nothing.
In which case he would need
to know nothing,
be responsible for nothing
and control nothing.

He would also be unhappy
and he definitely would be dead
so far as himself
and all else was concerned.
But, as you can't kill a thetan,
the state is impossible to maintain
and the road back
can be gruesome.

Management Series: "The Top Triangle"

*A*ll overt acts
are the product of irresponsibility
on one or more of the dynamics.

Technical Bulletin: "Justification"

*S*laves are made
by giving them freedom
from responsibility.

Scientology 8-8008

One is as responsible
as one can communicate.
One is not responsible
for that with which
he cannot communicate.
One will fight only
that with which
he cannot communicate.

Scientology 8-8008

The way not to have
is to ignore or combat
or withdraw from.
These three, ignoring
or combating
or withdrawing,
sum up to no having.
They also sum up
to no responsibility
for such things.

Organization Executive Course: "Responsibility Again"

*Little by little
one can make anything go right by
increasing knowledge
on all dynamics,
increasing responsibility
on all dynamics,
increasing control
on all dynamics.*

Management Series: "The Top Triangle"

About the Author

About the Author

L. Ron Hubbard is one of the most acclaimed and widely read authors of all time, primarily because his works express a firsthand knowledge of the nature of man—knowledge gained not from standing on the sidelines but through lifelong experience with people from all walks of life.

As Ron said, "One doesn't learn about life by sitting in an ivory tower, thinking about it. One learns about life by being part of it." And that is how he lived.

He began his quest for knowledge on the nature of man at a very early age. When he was eight years old he was already well on his way to being a seasoned traveler. His adventures included voyages to China, Japan and other points in the Orient and South Pacific, covering a quarter of a million miles by the age of nineteen. In the course of his travels he became closely acquainted with twenty-one different races and cultures all over the world.

In the fall of 1930, Ron pursued his studies of mathematics and engineering, enrolling at George Washington University where he was also a member of one of the first American classes on nuclear physics. He realized that neither the East nor the West contained the full answer to the problems of existence. Despite all of mankind's advances in the physical sciences, a *workable* technology of the mind and life had never been developed. The mental "technologies" which did exist, psychology and psychiatry, were actually barbaric, false subjects—no more workable than the methods of jungle witch doctors. Ron shouldered the responsibility of filling this gap in the knowledge of mankind.

He financed his early research through fiction writing. He became one of the most highly demanded authors in the golden age of popular adventure and science fiction writing during the 1930s and 1940s, interrupted only by his service in the US Navy during World War II.

Partially disabled at the war's end, Ron applied what he had learned from his researches. He made breakthroughs and developed techniques which made it possible for him to recover from his injuries and help others to regain their health. It was during this time that the basic tenets of Dianetics technology were codified.

In late 1947, he wrote a manuscript detailing his discoveries. It was not published at that time, but circulated amongst Ron's friends, who copied it and passed it on to others. (This manuscript was formally published in 1951 as *Dianetics: The Original Thesis* and later republished as *The Dynamics of Life*.) The interest generated by this manuscript prompted a flood of requests for more information on the subject.

Ron provided all his discoveries to the American Psychiatric Association and the American Medical Association. Despite the fact that his work would have benefited them and society immensely, they ignored his research and continued on with their archaic activities.

Meanwhile, the steadily increasing flow of letters asking for further information and requesting that he detail more applications of his new subject resulted in Ron spending all his time answering letters. He decided to write and publish a comprehensive text on the subject—*Dianetics: The Modern Science of Mental Health*.

With the release of *Dianetics* on 9 May 1950, a complete handbook for the application of Ron's new technology was broadly available for the first time. Public interest spread like wildfire. The book shot to the top of the *New York Times* bestseller list and remained there week after week. More than 750 Dianetics study groups sprang up within a few months of its publication.

Ron's work did not stop with the success of *Dianetics* but accelerated, with new discoveries and breakthroughs a constant, normal occurrence. In his further research he discovered the very nature of life itself and its exact relationship to this universe. These discoveries led to his development of Scientology, the first workable technology for the improvement of conditions in any aspect of life. Scientology encompasses techniques which can help increase a person's success in his own personal relationships, at his work and in his day-to-day activities.

Through the 1960s, 70s and into the 80s, Ron continued his research and writing, amassing an enormous volume of material

totaling over 60 million words—recorded in books, manuscripts and taped lectures. Today these works are studied and applied daily in hundreds of Scientology churches, missions and organizations around the world.

With his research fully completed and codified, L. Ron Hubbard departed his body on 24 January 1986.

Ron's work opened a wide bridge to understanding and freedom for mankind. Through his efforts, there now exists a totally workable technology with which people can help each other improve their lives and succeed in achieving their goals.

Glossary

aberration: departure from rational thought or behavior. From the Latin, *aberrare,* to wander from; Latin, *ab,* away, *errare,* to wander. It means basically to err, to make mistakes, or more specifically to have fixed ideas which are not true. The word is also used in its scientific sense. It means departure from a straight line. If a line should go from A to B, then if it is "aberrated" it would go from A to some other point, to some other point, to some other point, to some other point, to some other point and finally arrive at B. Taken in its scientific sense, it would also mean the lack of straightness or to see crookedly as, in example, a man sees a horse but thinks he sees an elephant. Aberrated conduct would be wrong conduct, or conduct not supported by reason. *Aberration* is opposed to sanity, which would be its opposite. *It takes unknowingness, joined to a game condition, to bring about aberration.*

aberrative: tending toward or capable of causing aberration in a person. See also **aberration** in this glossary. *It is the unknown incident which is the aberrative incident.*

absolute: something that is not dependent upon external conditions for existence or for its specific nature, size, etc. (opposed to *relative*—something that *is* dependent on external conditions for its nature, size, etc.). *Space, then, is not an arbitrary and absolute but it is creatable or uncreatable by a viewpoint.*

aesthetic: having to do with the beautiful, as distinguished from the useful, scientific, etc. Theta favors an aesthetic band because that's closest in to motionlessness; it's closest in to the fine wavelength which can append to theta itself.

affinity: degree of liking or affection or lack of it. Affinity is a tolerance of distance. A great affinity would be a tolerance of or liking of close proximity. A lack of affinity would be an intolerance of or dislike of close proximity. Affinity is one of the components of understanding. Theta, the energy of thought and life, has as primary manifestations affinity, reality and communication.

alloyed: weakened or spoiled through the addition of something that reduces value or pleasure. Never permit your affinity to be alloyed.

alter-isness: the state, quality or instance of altering or changing the reality of something. Isness means the way it is. When someone sees it differently he is doing an alter-is; in other words, is altering the way it is. For more information, see the Scientology Axioms in the book *Scientology 0-8: The Book of Basics* by L. Ron Hubbard. Lying becomes alter-isness, becomes stupidity.

amour: (French) love. It is enjoyment of work, contemplation of deeds well done; it is a good book or a good friend; it is taking all the skin off one's knees climbing the Matterhorn; it is hearing the kid first say "Daddy"; it is a brawl on the Bund at Shanghai or the whistle of amour from a doorway; it's adventure and hope and enthusiasm and "someday I'll learn to paint"; it's eating a good meal or kissing a pretty girl or playing a stiff game of bluff on the stock exchange.

animating: giving life to; making alive. *Life is a static which yet has the power of controlling, animating, mobilizing, organizing and destroying matter, energy and space and possibly even time.*

antipathetic: opposed or antagonistic in character, tendency, etc. *Children out of present time, bent on revenge, fresh from a quarrelsome breakfast table in an antipathetic home form a noisy and rebellious group.*

arbitrary: something which is introduced into a situation without regard to the data of the situation. *Space, then, is not an arbitrary and absolute but it is creatable or uncreatable by a viewpoint.*

ARC: a word made from the initial letters of Affinity, Reality and Communication which together equate to understanding. These are the three things necessary to the understanding of something—one has to have some affinity for it, it has to be real to him to some degree and he needs some communication with it before he can understand it. For more information on ARC, read the book *The Problems of Work* by L. Ron Hubbard. See also **affinity, reality** and **communication** in this glossary. *[Title: On ARC]*

arduous: involving great hardship or exertion; difficult. *Play was seen to be something that was interesting and work was seen to be something that was arduous and necessary and therefore not interesting.*

Aristotle: (384–322 B.C.) Greek philosopher noted for his works on logic, ethics, politics, etc. *Unless you can test and establish the truth and value of the data being used, one cannot attain right answers no matter what Aristotle may have said or what IBM may have built.*

art: (1) archaic form of the word "are"; used with *thou*. *See also* **thou** in this glossary. *Thou Shalt Have No Force Nor Illusion Nor Thine Own Placement or Knowingness in Space and Time for All Illusion Is Mine and If Thou Art I Shall Not Be.*
(2) creative work or its principles; making or doing of things that display form, beauty and unusual perception: art includes painting, sculpture, architecture, music, literature, drama, the dance, etc. *Reason, analytical waves, are too coarse to attain theta's zero or infinity "wavelength." Art alone may do so.*

as-ised: caused to vanish or cease to exist. This is accomplished by viewing something exactly as it is, without any distortions or lies. For more information, see the Scientology Axioms in *Scientology 0-8: The Book of Basics* by L. Ron Hubbard. *Freedom cannot be erased. A static cannot be as-ised.*

assimilated: absorbed and incorporated into (made part of) one's thinking. *Study it with the purpose in mind of arriving at his own conclusions as to whether or not the tenets he has assimilated are correct and workable.*

auditing: another word for *processing,* the application of Dianetics or Scientology processes to someone by a trained auditor. *See also* **processing** in this glossary. [Reference: *Organization Executive Course: "The Big Auditing Problem"*]

auditor: a person trained and qualified in applying Dianetics and/or Scientology processes and procedures to individuals for their betterment; called an auditor because *auditor* means *one who listens. See also*

processing in this glossary. *[Definition of PAB] Their intent was to give the professional auditor and his preclears the best possible processes and processing available at the moment it became available.*

authoritarian: believing in, relating to or characterized by unquestioning obedience to an expert on a subject. *As a society declines, it more and more resorts to authoritarian teaching and attempts increasingly to impress upon the individual that he must adjust to his environment and that he cannot adjust his environment to him.*

automaticity: something one is doing but is unaware or only partially aware he is doing; something the individual has "on automatic." *An automaticity is something which ought to be under the control of the individual, but isn't. And it becomes an automaticity—a game going on below the level of knowingness.*

band: range; level. Used here in reference to a particular range of wavelengths. *Theta favors an aesthetic band because that's closest in to motionlessness; it's closest in to the fine wavelength which can append to theta itself.*

bank: the mental image picture collection of the preclear—the reactive mind. It comes from computer terminology where all data is in a "bank." See also **mental image picture** and **reactive mind** in this glossary. *If you reduce a man's effort output to zero you will also collapse his bank on him.*

barbarism: a barbarous (uncultured, uncivilized, unpolished) social or intellectual condition; absence of culture; uncivilized ignorance and rudeness. *If all the workmen in America and England became unwilling to work, one would again see a barbarism.*

being certainness: state, quality or instance of being certain or having no doubt; state of being sure or positive. *Knowingness is being certainness.*

beingness: the assumption or choosing of a category of identity. Beingness is assumed by oneself or given to oneself or is attained. Examples of beingness would be one's own name, one's profession, one's physical characteristics, one's role in a game—each and all of these things could be called one's beingness. *The whole business of knowingness is beingness.*

bent: determined; set; resolved. *The little child is quite bent on causing effects and getting things admired.*

blow-offs: a colloquialism (informal expression) for sudden departures. It is usually used to describe someone leaving or ceasing to be where he should really be. *[Reference:* **Technical Bulletin:** *"Blow-Offs"]*

blows off: suddenly dissipates (disperses; vanishes). *When you start to introduce order into anything, disorder shows up and blows off.*

Bund: internationally famous waterfront section of the port district in Shanghai. *See also* **Shanghai** *in this glossary. It is enjoyment of work, contemplation of deeds well done; it is a good book or a good friend; it is taking all the skin off one's knees climbing the Matterhorn; it is hearing the kid first say "Daddy"; it is a brawl on the Bund at Shanghai or the whistle of amour from a doorway; it's adventure and hope and enthusiasm and "someday I'll learn to paint"; it's eating a good meal or kissing a pretty girl or playing a stiff game of bluff on the stock exchange.*

capitalists: advocates of *capitalism*, the economic system in which all or most of the means of production and distribution, as land, factories, railroads, etc., are privately owned and operated for profit, originally under fully competitive conditions: it has been generally characterized by a tendency toward concentration of wealth, and, in its later phase, by the growth of great corporations, increased governmental control, etc. *In 1870 we find capitalists resisting Marx.*

case: a person's mental condition. *A person's case is the way he responds to the world around him by reason of his aberrations. See also* **aberration** *in this glossary. [Reference: Technical Bulletin: "The Circuit Case"]*

case gain: the improvements and resurgences a person experiences from auditing; any case betterment according to the preclear. *See also* **case** *in this glossary. Above case gain is* **competence.**

chaos: total disorder or confusion. *Lacking any one of these skills, for they are skills, no matter how native they are to the individual, one is apt to get into a chaos of thinkingness or creatingness or livingness.*

circuit: a part of an individual's mind that behaves as though it were someone or something separate from him and that either talks to him or goes into action of its own accord, and may even, if severe enough, take control of him while it operates. *[Reference: Technical Bulletin: "The Circuit Case"]*

clandestinely: in a secret or hidden manner, especially for some purpose; not properly or lawfully. *A "love" clandestinely conducted and based on lies which will bring harm to others denotes a cowardice low enough to bring nausea to any decent man.*

Clear: the name of a state achieved through auditing or an individual who has achieved this state. A Clear is a being who no longer has his own reactive mind. A Clear is an unaberrated person and is rational in that he forms the best possible solutions he can on the data he has and from his viewpoint. *See also* **reactive mind** *and* **aberration** *in this glossary.* [*Reference: Lecture: "Clear Procedure"*]

cleared: having been brought, through auditing, to the state of Clear. *See also* **Clear** *in this glossary. The thetan is a knowingness, total in a cleared state, who yet can create space and time and objects to locate in them.*

comm: short for *communication. See also* **communication** *in this glossary. Truth has comm value.*

communication: the interchange of ideas across space. Its full definition is the consideration and action of impelling an impulse or particle from source-point across a distance to receipt-point, with the intention of bringing into being at the receipt-point a duplication and understanding of that which emanated from the source-point. The formula of communication is cause, distance, effect, with intention, attention and duplication with understanding. *All unknown is, is out of communication.*

concentration camp: a camp where prisoners of war, enemy aliens and political prisoners are confined. Used figuratively. *Resistance and restraint are the barbed wire of this concentration camp.*

corollary: a natural consequence or result; something that follows logically after something else is proved. *Corollary: A universe is affected only by the postulates of the god of that universe.*

counsel, keep your own: don't open up your thoughts, plans, etc., to deliberation and discussion by others. *Be your own adviser, keep your own counsel and select your own decisions.*

creatingness: state, quality or instance of creating. *Lacking any one of these skills, for they are skills, no matter how native they are to the individual, one is apt to get into a chaos of thinkingness or creatingness or livingness.*

cuff, off the: (slang) without preparation; in an offhand manner. *There is only slavery when nobody knows and the rules are all "off the cuff."*

cult: a group showing an obsessive devotion to a person, principle or ideal. *Today we live in a vast cult called "Worship the body."*

cut above, a: (informal) somewhat superior to another (thing, person, etc.) in some respect. *They are a cut above man.*

democracy: government in which the people hold the ruling power either directly or through elected representatives; rule by the ruled. *It is impossible to have a working democracy without its ranks including only intelligent and capable individuals.*

deprave: make morally bad; corrupt. *A government wishing to deprave its people to the point where they will accept the most perfidious and rotten acts, abolishes first the concept of God, and in the wake of that destroys the family with "free love," the intellectual with police-enforced idiocies, and so reduces a whole population to an estate somewhat below that of dogs.*

Dianetics: Dianetics spiritual healing technology. It addresses and handles the effects of the spirit on the body and can alleviate such things as unwanted sensations and emotions, accidents, injuries and psychosomatic illnesses (ones that are caused or aggravated by mental stress). *Dianetics* means "through the soul" (from Greek *dia*, through, and *nous*, soul). It is further defined as "what the soul is doing to the body." [Reference: *The Route to Infinity Lectures: Appendix, "Dianetics Jingles"*]

dilettante: a person who follows an art or science only for amusement and in a superficial way; dabbler. The dilettante has no technique, and so he only plays the role of the artist.

discourse: communication of ideas, information, etc., especially by talking; conversation. Thus we have friendly discourse high on the scale and war at the bottom.

disposition: arrangement or distribution. The essential definition of having is to be able to touch or permeate or to direct the disposition of.

divergent: differing from each other. Any field which has critics galore, wherein a thousand different schools of divergent opinion can exist, where opinion is listened to with open mouths in lieu of reason by which any man can reach a conclusion, is an authoritarian field.

docility: submissiveness to training or management; quality of being easily managed or controlled. One can go along in the numb world of the middle class watching his public docility while he hypocritically sins behind doors and conforms with a capital C.

down pat: mastered or learned perfectly. *When you think of uncertainty, stupidity and insecurity, think of confusion and you'll have it down pat.*

dramatizing: repeating in action what has happened to one in experience; replaying now something that happened then. *Dramatization is the duplication of the content of a mental image picture, entire or in part, by a person in his present time environment. See also* **mental image picture** *in this glossary. Dramatizing is an apology for failure.*

duplication: the act of something being made, done or happening again. *In Scientology, duplication is also used to describe the action of reproducing something exactly. For example, if Person A communicated the concept of a cat to Person B and Person B got the exact same concept of a cat without any alteration, Person B would be said to have duplicated what was originated by Person A. Duplication is thus difficult.*

duress: the use of force or threats; compulsion. *Too much agreement under duress brings about the vanishment of one's entire consciousness.*

dynamic: the surge of energy within an individual which is seeking to promote survival. *The persistency of the individual in life is directly governed by the strength of his basic dynamic.*

dynamics: the eight urges (drives, impulses) in life. They are motives or motivations. We call them the eight dynamics. These are urges for survival as or through (1) self, (2) sex and family, (3) groups, (4) all mankind, (5) living things (plants and animals), (6) the material universe, (7) spirits, and (8) infinity or the Supreme Being. *Universes are created by the application of self-determinism on eight dynamics.*

effect: the receipt point of an idea, particle or mass. Therefore, the person who catches a baseball thrown at him is being an effect. At that moment he's an effect, the person who threw the baseball is cause. The person being "educated" is, day after day, immobilized, made into an effect by instructors and denied original thought.

empirical: derived from or guided by experience or experiment. It is an empirical observation that men without a strong and lasting faith in a Supreme Being are less capable, less ethical and less valuable to themselves and society.

entheta: (1) theta which is enturbulated with MEST in an inharmonious combination. Irrational thought. *See also* **MEST** in this glossary. Theta crushed too hard into MEST becomes entheta.
(2) enturbulated theta (thought or life); especially referring to communications, which, based on lies and confusions, are slanderous, choppy or destructive in an attempt to overwhelm or suppress a person or group. While it may be true that something is undesirable or that a person is bad, if it serves no good purpose to make the statement, the issuance of this "truth" is in reality the establishing of an entheta line.

entity: being or existence, especially when considered as distinct, independent or self-contained. Any knowledge which can be sensed, measured, experienced, by any entity is capable of influencing that entity.

enturbulated: turbulent or agitated and disturbed. It is an aspect of theta that the more it is enturbulated the easier it is to enter enturbulence into it.

environ: abbreviation for *environment,* one's surroundings; the material things around one; the area one lives in; the living things, objects, spaces and forces with which one lives whether close to or far away. Or one can simply confront the whole thing, pain, misemotion, punishments, rewards and all and produce and exchange and learn to handle the administrative system he is in and himself administer his life and environ.

equilibrium: a state of rest or balance due to the equal action of opposing forces. A static has no motion; it has no width, length, breadth, depth; it is not held in suspension by an equilibrium of forces; it does not have mass; it does not contain wavelengths; it has no situation in time or space.

estate: condition or circumstances with reference to worldly prosperity, estimation, etc.; social status or rank. A government wishing to deprave its people to the point where they will accept the most perfidious and rotten acts, abolishes first the concept of God, and in the wake of that destroys the family with "free love," the intellectual with police-enforced idiocies, and so reduces a whole population to an estate somewhat below that of dogs.

ethic: having to do with ethics or morality; of or conforming to ethical standards. *See also* **ethics** in this glossary. A culture is as rich and as capable of surviving as it has imaginative artists, skilled men of science, a high ethic level, workable government, land and natural resources, in about that order of importance.

ethics: rationality toward the highest level of survival for the individual, the future race, the group and mankind. Ethics is reason and the contemplation of optimum survival. A system of ethics exists in Scientology whereby a person can take certain actions to correct some

conduct or situation in which he is involved which is contrary to the ideals and best interests of his group. Ethics consists simply of the actions an individual takes on himself. It is a personal thing. When one is ethical or "has his ethics in," it is by his own choice and is done by himself. *Ethics are reason.*

eventualities: possible events, outcomes or conditions. *If we cannot imagine eventualities, we cannot prevent future failures.*

fabric: framework or basic structure of anything. *No society can exist on a fabric of slaves.*

facsimile: a recording in energy of an incident or part of an incident from the past. The facsimile contains all the perceptics of the original. It is an involuntary duplicate or copy (*not a perfect duplicate*). *Thought is the phenomenon of combining, imagining or postulating theta facsimiles for the estimation of future physical efforts.*

ferocity: ferocious quality or state; savage fierceness. *Despite its ferocity, the universe is at best an illusion, if a very solid one.*

fixation: a concentration on one idea; an obsession. *This world is full of the "noise" of many lies, many babbles, many old fixations and hates.*

foibles: minor weaknesses or failings of character; slight flaws or defects. *The ability to arrange life and the environment so that living can be better enjoyed, the ability to tolerate the foibles of one's fellow humans, the ability to see the true factors in a situation and resolve problems of living with accuracy, the ability to accept and execute responsibility, these things are important.*

folly: a lack of sense or sensible conduct; foolishness. *It is folly to try to control something or even know something without responsibility.*

footlights: a row of lights at the front of a stage, nearly on a level with the feet of the actors. *You can't stand bowing back of the footlights forever with no show even if you are quite an actor.*

foregone conclusion: a conclusion, opinion or decision formed in advance of proper consideration of evidence, arguments, etc. *Do not allow the authority of any one person or school of thought to create a foregone conclusion within your sphere of knowledge.*

forthright: direct and without evasion; straightforward. *There are those who talk about "lucky breaks" and who speak of the "hand of fate" in their undertakings, but a forthright examination of the field of man's activities will show that nearly all success is most adequately deserved.*

garbs: covers with or as if with clothing; dresses. Used figuratively. *When one loses the illusion of one's dreams, when one no longer garbs one's none-too-brilliant history and rather perishable body with illusion, life, bluntly and brutally, isn't worth living.*

gnome: (folklore) any of a race of small, misshapen, dwarflike beings, supposed to dwell in the earth and guard its treasures. *And if this were all there were to surviving and if necessity were a vicious little gnome with a pitchfork, it seems rather obvious that there would be scant reason to go on living.*

grace: elegance or beauty of form, manner, motion or action. *A little child derives all of his pleasure in life from the grace he puts upon life.*

grind: laborious, usually uninteresting work. But when we have our vacations and go and "play" we are usually very glad to get back to the "daily grind."

hat: the title and work of a post (job), taken from the fact that in many professions, such as railroading, the type of hat worn is the badge of the job. The term *hat* is also used to describe the write-ups, checksheets and packs that outline the purposes, know-how and duties of a post. It exists in folders and packs and is trained in on the person on the post. *When a person has no hat he lacks purpose and value.*

havingness: the concept of being able to reach. By havingness we mean owning, possessing, being capable of commanding, taking charge of objects, energies and spaces. *Games require space and havingness.*

HCO: abbreviation for *Hubbard Communications Office:* the division of a Scientology organization which is responsible for the hiring of personnel, routing of incoming and outgoing communications and maintaining ethics and justice among Scientologists on staff and in the area. See also **ethics** in this glossary. *[Definition of HCOB] abbreviation for Hubbard Communications Office Bulletin: a technical issue written by L. Ron Hubbard only.*

HCOB: abbreviation for *Hubbard Communications Office Bulletin:* a technical issue written by L. Ron Hubbard only. An HCOB is valid from first issue unless specifically cancelled. All data for auditing and courses is contained in HCOBs. These outline the product of the organization. They are issued in red ink on white paper, consecutive by date. See also **auditing** and **HCO** in this glossary. *[Bibliography: Art and Communication, HCOB 26 Sept. 77R.]*

HCO Exec Ltr: short for *HCO Executive Letter,* a type of issue which was written by L. Ron Hubbard between 1964 and 1966, and contained direct executive orders or requests for reports or data or news or merely information. *[Reference: Justice, HCO Exec Ltr 18 Mar. 65]*

HCO PL: abbreviation for *Hubbard Communications Office Policy Letter:* a permanently valid issue of organization and administrative technology. HCO PLs, regardless of date or age, form the know-how of running an organization or group or company. These make up the bulk of staff hat materials in Scientology organizations. HCO PLs are signed by L. Ron Hubbard and issued in green ink on white paper, consecutive by date. *See also* **hat** *and* **HCO** *in this glossary. [Bibliography: Artistic Presentation, HCO PL 8 Oct. 64]*

hectically: in a confused, rushed, excited, etc., manner. *People seek happiness in various ways, hectically, seriously, desperately; but the odd part of it is that they find only what they themselves put there.*

hitherto: up to this time; until now. *The thetan is immortal and is possessed of capabilities well in excess of those hitherto predicted for man.*

hobo: a person who wanders about and lives by begging or doing odd jobs; tramp. *One may float along on the production of others like the recently demised "leisure class" of 19th century infamy or like a hobo being chased by every householder and cop.*

Homo novis: literally, new man, from the Latin *Homo,* man, and *novus,* new. *[Reference: Article: "The Limitations of Homo Novis"]*

householder: one who owns or maintains a house. *One may float along on the production of others like the recently demised "leisure class" of*

19th century infamy or like a hobo being chased by every householder and cop.

humbleness: the condition of having or showing an awareness of one's weaknesses and faults; modesty. *Beginning to know that one doesn't know is not a lesson in humbleness but one in wisdom.*

hypocritically: in the manner of one who pretends to have desirable or publicly approved attitudes, beliefs, principles, etc., he does not actually possess. *One can go along in the numb world of the middle class watching his public docility while he hypocritically sins behind doors and conforms with a capital C.*

IBM: International Business Machines Corporation, a leading US business machine and computer manufacturer. *Unless you can test and establish the truth and value of the data being used, one cannot attain right answers no matter what Aristotle may have said or what IBM may have built.*

immobilized: prevented from movement. *The person being "educated" is, day after day, immobilized, made into an effect by instructors and denied original thought.*

infamy: very bad reputation; disgrace or dishonor. *One may float along on the production of others like the recently demised "leisure class" of 19th century infamy or like a hobo being chased by every householder and cop.*

inflation: an increase in the amount of money and credit in relation to the supply of goods and services, resulting in an increase in the general price level. *An inflation exists where there is more money in*

circulation than there are goods. *As slavery increases in a country, as freedom becomes less, inflation and other economic evils become more because slave peoples do not produce and free peoples do.*

irresolute: wavering in decision, purpose or opinion; indecisive. *Worry is constant, irresolute computation—constant computation on a certain point or a certain problem.*

jingles: verses or tunes that have obvious, easy rhythm, simple rhymes, etc. The "Dianetics Jingles" have been published in *Technical Bulletins Volume I* and as an appendix to *The Route to Infinity* lecture series transcripts. [Reference: **The Route to Infinity Lectures:** *Appendix,* "*Dianetics Jingles*"]

kilotons: measurements of explosive force equal to that of 1,000 tons of TNT. *The power (defined as light-year kilotons per microsecond) of a thetan is measured by nothing else than the distance (defined as spherical spatial length) around him in his environment that he can control.*

kindled: aroused or excited (interest, feelings, etc.) *Interest is mainly kindled by the unpredictable.*

knowingness: awareness not depending upon perception. One doesn't have to look to find out. For example, you do not have to get a perception or picture of where you are living to know where you live. *Knowingness itself is certainty.*

learned: of or characterized by scholarship, study and learning. *The basic definition of sanity in this somewhat nebulously learned society is whether or not a person agrees with everyone else.*

light-year: *(astronomy)* of a unit of distance equal to the distance that light travels in a vacuum in one year, approximately six trillion miles. *The power (defined as light-year kilotons per microsecond) of a thetan is measured by nothing else than the distance (defined as spherical spatial length) around him in his environment that he can control.*

livingness: the activity of going along a certain course, impelled (driven) by a purpose and with some place to arrive. *Lacking any one of these skills, for they are skills, no matter how native they are to the individual, one is apt to get into a chaos of thinkingness or creatingness or livingness.*

lore: knowledge or learning; specifically all the knowledge of a particular group or having to do with a particular subject. *Every bit of scientific lore which has been accumulated by scientists in the hope that it may better the lot of their fellow men has eventually been employed in the destruction of men.*

lot: position in life; fortune. *Every bit of scientific lore which has been accumulated by scientists in the hope that it may better the lot of their fellow men has eventually been employed in the destruction of men.*

lots: great numbers or amounts. *Man alone of the animal and vegetable kingdom possesses the potential power of changing MEST in wholesale lots into something theta can use.*

manifestation: the demonstration, revelation or display of the existence, presence, qualities or nature of some person or thing. *Seek for the* reasons behind a manifestation, and postulate the manner and in which direction the manifestation will likely proceed.

Marx: Karl Marx (1818–1883) German political philosopher. Regarded by some as founder of modern socialism. The work he is most known for is *The Communist Manifesto* in which he states that the evils of capitalist society cannot be abolished by reform, but only by the destruction of the whole capitalist economy and establishment of a new classless society. *In 1870 we find capitalists resisting Marx.*

Matterhorn: one of the best-known mountains (14,782 ft.) in the Alps, on the frontier between Switzerland and Italy, frequently ascended by mountain climbers in summer. *It is enjoyment of work, contemplation of deeds well done; it is a good book or a good friend; it is taking all the skin off one's knees climbing the Matterhorn; it is hearing the kid first say "Daddy"; it is a brawl on the Bund at Shanghai or the whistle of amour from a doorway; it's adventure and hope and enthusiasm and "someday I'll learn to paint"; it's eating a good meal or kissing a pretty girl or playing a stiff game of bluff on the stock exchange.*

mechanical definition: a statement of something defined in terms of distance and position. Mechanical in this sense means interpreting or explaining the phenomena of the universe by referring to physical forces; mechanistic. Thus a *mechanical definition* would be one which defined in terms of space or location such as "the car over by the old oak tree" or "the man who lives in the big house." Here "the old oak tree" and "the big house" are fixed objects and the unfixed objects

("car," "man") are a sort of viewpoint. One has identified things by location. *Mechanical definition: Stupidity is unknownness of time, place, form and event.*

mechanics: the functional and technical aspects of an activity. The mechanics of perception consist of putting something out there and then wondering what it is.

memory bank: the total of a person's memories or recollections. There is no knowledge worth knowing that's in your memory bank.

mental image picture: a mental copy of one's perceptions sometime in the past; a three-dimensional color picture with sound and smell and all other perceptions, plus the conclusions or speculations of the individual. For example, if a person was in a car accident, he would retain "pictures" of that experience in his mind, complete with recordings of the sights, physical sensations, smells, sounds, etc., that occurred during that incident. For further information on mental image pictures and how the mind works, read *Dianetics: The Modern Science of Mental Health* by L. Ron Hubbard. [Definition of **bank:** the mental image picture collection of the preclear—the reactive mind.]

MEST: a word coined from the initial letters of *Matter, Energy, Space and Time,* which are the component parts (elements) of the physical universe. Also used as a noun to refer to the physical universe, and loosely to mean physical universe objects, such as property or possessions. One's appreciation of the MEST universe is almost uniformly the energy which one himself places upon the MEST universe, in other words his illusions.

microsecond: a unit of time equal to one-millionth of a second. *The power (defined as light-year kilotons per microsecond) of a thetan is measured by nothing else than the distance (defined as spherical spatial length) around him in his environment that the can control.*

mires: causes to get stuck in or as in mire (deep mud; wet, soggy earth). Used figuratively. *An evolution toward complexity is an evolution toward authoritarianism and pomposity—"You couldn't possibly understand this, therefore I, who pretend to, am important" is the attitude which mires learning.*

misemotion: a coined word used in Dianetics and Scientology to mean an emotion or emotional reaction that is inappropriate to the present time situation. It is taken from *mis-* (wrong) + *emotion.* To say that a person was *misemotional* would indicate that the person did not display the emotion called for by the actual circumstances of the situation. Being misemotional would be synonymous with being irrational. *One can fairly judge the rationality of any individual by the correctness of the emotion he displays in a given set of circumstances. To be joyful and happy when circumstances call for joy and happiness would be rational. To display grief without sufficient present time cause would be irrational. Or one can simply confront the whole thing, pain, misemotion, punishments, rewards and all and produce and exchange and learn to handle the administrative system he is in and himself administer his life and environ.*

mock up: as used here, it simply means "create." In Scientology, the *word mock up is used* to mean, in essence, something which a person makes up himself. A *mock-up* is more than a mental picture; it is a self-created object which exists as itself or symbolizes some object in the physical universe. The term was derived from the World War II phrase for miniature models that were constructed to symbolize weapons (airplanes, ships, artillery, etc.) or areas of attack (hills, rivers, buildings, etc.) for use in planning a battle. After an artist finishes a piece of work, whether it is a story or anything else, he should mock up the audience reading him.

modus operandi: *(Latin)* mode of operation; way of doing or making; procedure. *Communication is not only the modus operandi, it is the heart of life and is by thousands of percent the senior in importance to affinity and reality.*

monitor: oversee, supervise or regulate. *People monitor their existence by affinity.*

mystic: short for *mysticism,* the beliefs or practices of those who claim to have experiences based on intuition, meditation, etc., of a spiritual nature, by which they learn truths not known by ordinary people. *Those who gave us mystic were sadistic.*

nebulously: in a manner lacking form; hazily; vaguely; confusedly. *The basic definition of sanity in this somewhat nebulously learned society is whether or not a person agrees with everyone else.*

neurosis: a condition wherein a person is insane or disturbed on some subject (as opposed to psychosis, wherein a person is just insane in general). *In the absence of any basic training about neurosis, psychosis, or how to judge a good cook or a good wage earner, that tricky,* treacherous and not always easy-to-identify thing called "love" is the sole guiding factor in the selection of mates.

nurtured: helped to grow or develop; cultivated. *This relationship is the vessel wherein is nurtured the life force of both individuals, whereby they create the future of the race in body and thought.*

overt acts: acts by the person or individual leading to the injury, reduction or degradation of another, others or their persons, possessions or associations. An overt act can be intentional or unintentional. *The insane are just one seething mass of overt acts and withholds.*

over-the-ramparts: charging over or past one's own defenses. A rampart is an embankment of earth raised for defense against an enemy. *There is no substitute for an all-out, over-the-ramparts, howling charge against life.*

PAB: abbreviation for *Professional Auditor's Bulletin:* one of a series of issues written by L. Ron Hubbard between 10 May 1953 and 15 May 1959. The content of these bulletins is technical and promotional. Their intent was to give the professional auditor and his preclears the best possible processes and processing available at the moment it became available. *See also* **auditor** *and* **processing** *in this glossary.* [Bibliography: *Beingness and Certainty Processing, PAB 4, ca. June 53*]

paradox: a self-contradictory and false proposition. *An immortal being striving to survive presents immediately a paradox.*

parity: equality, as in amount, status, character. *There should be some parity of intellect and sanity between a husband and wife for them to have a successful marriage.*

perfidious: treacherous; disloyal. A government wishing to deprave its people to the point where they will accept the most perfidious and rotten acts, abolishes first the concept of God, and in the wake of that destroys the family with "free love," the intellectual with police-enforced idiocies, and so reduces a whole population to an estate somewhat below that of dogs.

persevere: persist in anything undertaken; maintain a purpose in spite of difficulty or obstacles; continue steadfastly. It stems from being true to one's own decency, from going on helping others whatever they do or think or say and despite all savage acts against one; to persevere without changing one's basic attitude toward man.

pomposity: the quality of being pompous, characterized by an exaggerated display of self-importance or dignity; boastfulness; arrogance. An evolution toward complexity is an evolution toward authoritarianism and pomposity—"You couldn't possibly understand this, therefore I, who pretend to, am important" is the attitude which mires learning.

post: a position, job or duty to which a person is assigned or appointed; an assigned area of responsibility and action in an organization which is supervised in part by an executive. A post or job is enormously valuable.

postulate: (1) put forward as a reality. Compare what you have learned with the known universe. Seek for the reasons behind a manifestation, and postulate the manner and in which direction the manifestation will likely proceed.

(2) that self-determined thought which starts, stops or changes past, present or future efforts; a conclusion, decision or resolution made by the individual himself to resolve a problem or set a pattern for the future or nullify a pattern of the past. Postulates are self-created truths. The postulate of a god of a universe is effective in that universe.

PR: an abbreviation for *public relations*, which is essentially the art of making good works well known. In Scientology slang, "PR" is used to mean putting up a lot of false reports to serve as a smoke screen for idleness or bad actions. *In a PR world, truth is the almost unknown commodity. This world is full of the "noise" of many lies, many babbles, many old fixations and hates.*

preclear: a spiritual being who is now on the road to becoming Clear, hence pre-Clear. *See also* **Clear** *in this glossary. If the preclear knows about it, it isn't aberrative.*

preponderance: greater number; greater weight; greater power or influence. *When the society at large is having a very rough time it contains a preponderance of individuals who cannot help and who cannot be helped.*

present time: the time which is now, rather than in the past or future. It is a term loosely applied to the environment existing in the present. A person said to be "out of present time" would be someone whose attention is fixed on past or future events to such an extent that he is not fully aware of or in communication with his actual present environment. *Looking into the past and looking into the extreme future, alike, are efforts to avoid present time and efforts to look elsewhere than at something.*

processing: the application of Dianetics and/or Scientology processes and procedures to individuals for their betterment. The exact definition of processing is: The action of asking a person a question (which he can understand and answer), getting an answer to that question and acknowledging him for that answer. *See also* **auditing** *in this glossary.* [Reference: *Technical Bulletin: "Future Processing"*]

progeny: children, descendants or offspring collectively. *When an individual is acting contrary to survival of himself, his group, progeny, race, mankind or life he can be considered to be unintelligent, uninformed or aberrated.*

provocations: acts that anger, enrage or exasperate. *And to love him despite all invitations to do otherwise, all provocations and all reasons why one should not.*

psychosis: any severe form of mental disorder; insanity. *In the absence of any basic training about neurosis, psychosis, or how to judge a good cook or a good wage earner, that tricky, treacherous and not always easy-to-identify thing called "love" is the sole guiding factor in the selection of mates.*

Q and A: (from "Question and Answer") in Scientology, a coined expression which means not getting an answer to one's question, failing to complete something, or deviating from an intended course of action. *Q and A is the disease of dodging life.*

randomity: a consideration of motion. *We have plus randomity and we have minus randomity. We can have, from the individual's consideration, too much or too little motion, or enough motion.*

What's enough motion measured by? The consideration of the individual. The term *randomity* is often used to mean simply too much motion or action. One obtains randomity by abandoning responsibility in some sphere. He will then find himself in conflict in that sphere.

rationality: the quality or condition of being rational; reasonableness or the possession or use of reason. *Ethics actually consist of rationality toward the highest level of survival for the individual, the future race, the group and mankind, and the other dynamics taken collectively.*

reactive: irrational, reacting instead of acting. *The artist injects the theta into the culture, and without that theta the culture becomes reactive.*

reactive mind: that portion of a person's mind which works on a totally stimulus-response basis, which is not under his volitional control and which exerts force and the power of command over his awareness, purposes, thoughts, body and actions. [Definition of *bank*: the mental image picture collection of the preclear—the reactive mind.]

reality: the solid objects, the real things of life; the degree of agreement reached by two people. *It is only when one confuses it with reality that one gets into trouble.*

Rembrandt: Harmensz van Rijn Rembrandt (1606–1669), Dutch painter and etcher; considered one of the greatest painters in history. *Compare, for example, Rembrandt and the dilettante.*

revelation: act of revealing, especially the disclosure of something not previously known or realized. *The least-free person is the person who cannot reveal his own acts and who protests the revelation of the improper acts of others.*

rheumatism: a popular term for any of the various painful conditions of the joints and muscles, characterized by inflammation, stiffness, etc. *Living does not consist of sitting in a temple in the shadows and getting rheumatism from the cold stones.*

rudiments: those steps or actions used to get the preclear in shape to be audited in that session. For auditing to take place at all the preclear must be "in-session" which means: (1) willing to talk to the auditor, (2) interested in own case. Rudiments are actions done to accomplish this. *[Reference: Technical Bulletin: "Goals in the Rudiments"]*

sadistic: deriving pleasure from inflicting physical or psychological pain on another or others. *Those who gave us mystic were sadistic.*

school of thought: a particular type of doctrine or practice, as followed by a body of persons. *Do not allow the authority of any one person or school of thought to create a foregone conclusion within your sphere of knowledge.*

Scientology: Scientology philosophy. It is the study and handling of the spirit in relationship to itself, universes and other life. Scientology means *scio*, knowing in the fullest sense of the word and *logos*, study. In itself the word means literally *knowing how to know.* Scientology is a "route," a way, rather than a dissertation or an assertive body of knowledge. Through its drills and studies one may find the truth for himself. The technology is therefore not expounded as something to believe, but something to do. *If any lesson is contained in Scientology, it is the lesson that the gates to all knowingness are open.*

seething: violently agitated or disturbed. *The insane are just one seething mass of overt acts and withholds.*

Selective Service: short for Selective Service System, the federal agency (in the United States) charged with the administration of compulsory military service. *A soldier shot on the field of battle may "blame" the sniper, Selective Service, the stupidity of government, but he nevertheless had full responsibility not only for being there and getting shot but for the sniper, Selective Service and the stupidity of government.*

self-determinism: power of choice; power of decision; ability to decide or determine the course of one's actions. *Reason and self-determinism are all but forbidden.*

shalt: (archaic) form of "shall"; used with *thou.* See also **thou** in this glossary. *Thou Shalt Have No Force Nor Illusion Nor Thine Own Placement or Knowingness in Space and Time for All Illusion Is Mine and If Thou Art I Shall Not Be.*

Shanghai: largest city of China and one of the world's greatest seaports. *It is enjoyment of work, contemplation of deeds well done; it is a good book or a good friend; it is taking all the skin off one's knees climbing the Matterhorn; it is hearing the kid first say "Daddy"; it is a brawl on the Bund at Shanghai or the whistle of amour from a doorway; it's adventure and hope and enthusiasm and "someday I'll learn to paint"; it's eating a good meal or kissing a pretty girl or playing a stiff game of bluff on the stock exchange.*

sniper: a person, especially a soldier, who shoots from a hidden position at individuals of an enemy force. *A soldier shot on the field of battle may "blame" the sniper, Selective Service, the stupidity of government, but he nevertheless had full responsibility not only for being there and*

getting shot but for the sniper, Selective Service and the stupidity of government.

splurge: indulge oneself in some luxury or pleasure. *Splurge on it!*

static: something which doesn't have wavelength, so it is not in motion; it doesn't have weight, it doesn't have mass, it doesn't have length, breadth or any of these things. It is motionlessness. *Life is a static which yet has the power of controlling, animating, mobilizing, organizing and destroying matter, energy and space and possibly even time.*

suspension: a state of being kept from falling, sinking, etc. *A static has no motion; it has no width, length, breadth, depth; it is not held in suspension by an equilibrium of forces; it does not have mass; it does not contain wavelengths; it has no situation in time or space.*

sway: sovereign power or authority; rule; dominion. *One's universe is an unthwarted sway, the MEST universe is a compromise.*

taxing: making difficult or excessive demands upon. *The only failure lies in taxing or pulling down the strength on which you depend.*

terminal: any thing that has mass and meaning; a point from which energy can flow or by which energy can be received. *When a game is done the player keeps around tokens. These are hopes the game will start again. When that hope is dead the token, the terminal, is hidden.*

theta: energy peculiar to life which acts upon material in the physical universe and animates it, mobilizes it and changes it; natural creative energy of a being which he has free to direct toward survival goals.

See also **thetan** *in this glossary. Thought is the phenomenon of combining, imagining or postulating theta facsimiles for the estimation of future physical efforts.*

thetan: the person himself—not his body or his name, the physical universe, his mind, or anything else; that which is aware of being aware; the identity which is the individual. The term was coined to eliminate any possible confusion with older, invalid concepts. It comes from the Greek letter *theta* (θ), which the Greeks used to represent *thought* or perhaps *spirit*, to which an *n* is added to make a noun in the modern style used to create words in engineering. It is also θ^n, or "theta to the nth degree," meaning unlimited or vast. The thetan is a knowingness, total in a cleared state, who yet can create space and time and objects to locate in them.

thin: lacking solidity, substance or vigor; slight, weak. Creative imagination can be such a complex computation and can be accomplished on such thin data by a good mind that it can assume an aspect of divine inspiration.

thine: (archaic) that or those belonging to thee (you). *Thou Shalt Have No Force Nor Illusion Nor Thine Own Placement or Knowingness in Space and Time for All Illusion Is Mine and If Thou Art I Shall Not Be.*

thinkingness: the state or condition of thinking and trying to figure out the reason for this and the reason for that, so much that one is not really looking at what is around him. Lacking any one of these skills, for they are skills, no matter how native they are to the individual, one is apt to get into a chaos of thinkingness or creatingness or livingness.

thou: *(archaic)* you. *Thou Shalt Have No Force Nor Illusion Nor Thine Own Placement or Knowingness in Space and Time for All Illusion Is Mine and If Thou Art I Shall Not Be.*

tolls: rings (as in a church bell) slowly with regularly repeated strokes, especially for announcing a death. *One does not send to find for whom the bell tolls without full willingness to have tolled it and to have caused the cause of its tolling.*

tone: a level of emotion as given on the Tone Scale. *See also* **Tone Scale** in this glossary. *If tone is to soar, create even more.*

Tone Scale: a scale, in Scientology, which shows the emotional tones of a person. These, ranged from the highest to the lowest, are, in part, serenity, enthusiasm (as we proceed downward), conservatism, boredom, antagonism, anger, covert hostility, fear, grief, apathy. An arbitrary numerical value is given to each level on the scale. There are many aspects of the Tone Scale and using it makes possible the prediction of human behavior. For further information on the Tone Scale, read the book *Self Analysis* by L. Ron Hubbard. *Education which invites and stimulates reason and seeks to accelerate the individual toward a successful and happy level of existence, and has enough faith in individuals to assume the good usage of the education, raises the individual on the Tone Scale.*

transpire: bring to pass; cause to happen. *If beauty you desire, beauty transpire.*

troth: one's pledged word; promise. *Agreement to what ought to be and then a shattering of the troth works all the spell that's needed for a recipe of misery.*

two-way communication: a two-way cycle of communication. For example: Joe, having originated a communication and having completed it, may then wait for Bill to originate a communication to Joe, thus completing the remainder of the two-way cycle of communication. Thus we get the normal cycle of a communication between two people. *See also* **communication** *in this glossary. When a work of painting, music or other form attains two-way communication, it is truly art.*

ultimate: most basic; fundamental; primary. *Life was busy teaching somebody a lesson, and the lesson it succeeded in teaching him was not to do any more living; and that ultimate lesson, then, was always at the base of education as it was done, so that education itself could be considered uberrative.*

unit: any magnitude regarded as an independent whole; a single, indivisible entity. *Life is a unit energy source.*

unthwarted: unhindered, not obstructed. *One's universe is an unthwarted sway, the* MEST *universe is a compromise.*

vessel: something regarded as a holder or receiver of something, especially something nonmaterial. *This relationship is the vessel wherein is nurtured the life force of both individuals, whereby they create the future of the race in body and thought.*

viewpoint: a point from which to view. Any being is a viewpoint; he is as much a being as he is able to assume viewpoints. *The universes, then, are three in number: the universe created by one viewpoint, the universe created by every other viewpoint, the universe created by the*

mutual action of viewpoints which is agreed to be upheld—the physical universe.

wavelength: (*physics*) the distance between any two corresponding points on a wave, measured along the line of travel of the wave. *A static has no motion; it has no width, length, breadth, depth; it is not held in suspension by an equilibrium of forces; it does not have mass; it does not contain wavelengths; it has no situation in time or space.*

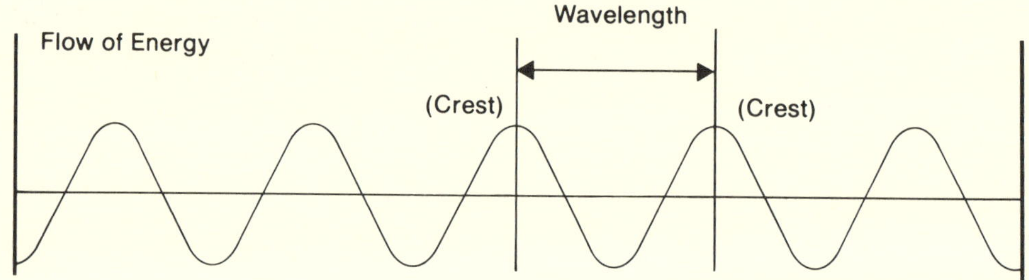

wax: grow or become. *Wax enthusiastic and you'll very soon feel so.*

whip: (*figurative*) compulsion or urging, as by whipping or flogging with a strap or rod. *It is better to be able to decide and control a few things to be, than to be under the whip of an imagination which drives one to be a great many things, none of which are under one's control.*

wholesale: in large quantities; on a large scale, especially without discrimination. *Man alone of the animal and vegetable kingdom possesses the potential power of changing MEST in wholesale lots into something theta can use.*

withholds: unspoken, unannounced transgressions against a moral code by which the person was bound. Things the person did that he or she is not talking about. A withhold is always the manifestation which comes after an overt. Any withhold comes after an overt. *See also* **overt acts** *in this glossary. The insane are just one seething mass of overt acts and withholds.*

Index

agreement, *(cont.)*

    MEST universe is that upon which one agrees in
        order to continue in association with
        other viewpoints, 89

    reality is, 186

    there is no trick to being unless you spend your
        time agreeing, 174

    time is created, at least in this universe, by
        creating energy and objects, and by being
        able to make the universe agree with
        oneself, not by having the universe
        continually making one agree
        with it, 138

    too much agreement under duress brings about
        the vanishment of one's entire
        consciousness, 186

    to rules and penalties, 338

    to what ought to be and then a shattering of
        the troth works all the spell that's needed
        for a recipe of misery, 271

alive, individual is as alive as he has ideas, 44

always, the real way to be assured of a great deal
    of time is to be able, of course, to create
    time, and this would be to a thetan the true
    concept of always, 141

amnesia, on a grand scale, 414

answer(s),

    depend on *data*, 82

    logic concerns obtaining answers, 82

    unless you can test and establish the truth and
        value of the data being used, one cannot
        attain right answers no matter what
        Aristotle may have said or what IBM
        may have built, 82

anxiety, can exist only in the presence of poor
    observation or the inability to observe, 6

appreciation,

    artist's most solid guarantee of, 154

    one's appreciation of the MEST universe is almost
        uniformly the energy which one himself
        places upon the MEST universe, in other
        words his illusions, 47

approval, never need praise, approval or
    sympathy, 448

ARC,

    in order to have an understanding of yourself,
        you must have good ARC with
        yourself, 198

    interactive triangle, 182

    person who is sane has a high ARC value, 199

    total knowingness would consist of total
        ARC, 197

arrogance, may win dominion and control but
    will never win acceptance and respect, 362

art,

    after an artist finishes a piece of work, whether
        it is a story or anything else, he should
        mock up the audience reading him; this is
        really his most solid guarantee of any
        appreciation, 154

    dilettante has no technique, and so he only
        plays the role of the artist, 153

    is the result of integration of all its components;
        one can add that the result invites
        contribution of and from the
        beholder, 151

    it is a relief to participate in predictable rhythm
        in an art form, 150

    professional knows the rules of the game as a
        matter of course so that he can achieve,
        in the upper strata above that, a high
        quality of art, 155

art, *(cont.)*

reason, analytical waves, are too coarse
to attain theta's zero or infinity
"wavelength"; art alone may
do so, 147

the opinion of the viewpoint regulates the
consideration of the forms, their
stillness or their motion, and these
considerations consist of assignment
of beauty or ugliness to the forms
and these considerations alone are
art, 157

we instinctively revere the great artist,
painter or musician and society as a
whole looks upon them as not quite
ordinary beings, 148

when a work of painting, music or other form
attains two-way communication, it is
truly art, 149

artist(s), *see also* **art**

culture is as rich and as capable of surviving as
it has imaginative artists, skilled men of
science, a high ethic level, workable
government, land and natural resources,
in about that order of importance, 237

injects the theta into the culture, and
without that theta the culture becomes
reactive, 228

association, is the essence of logic, 81

atomic war, if anything will kill Western society,
it is either tremendous political blunders
which bring about an atomic war, or this
philosophy that work is too hard to
confront, 379

attitude, life does not change so much as our
attitude toward it, 425

authoritarian(s)(ism),

an evolution toward complexity is an
evolution toward authoritarianism and
pomposity, 35

any field which has critics galore, wherein a
thousand different schools of divergent
opinion can exist, where opinion is
listened to with open mouths in lieu of
reason by which any man can reach a
conclusion, is an authoritarian field, 146

as a society declines, it more and more resorts
to authoritarian teaching, 30

do not achieve any results beyond their own
satisfaction, 36

authority,

acceptance of data and, 294

belongs to those who can *do* the task in any
given field, 38

awareness,

if one can confront, he can be aware, 14

increased awareness is the only factor which
offers any road out, 13

individual is as aware as he has ideas, 44

bank, if you reduce a man's effort output to zero
you will also collapse his bank on him, 369

barbarism, if all the workmen in America and
England became unwilling to work, one
would again see a barbarism, 394

beauty,

if beauty you desire, beauty transpire, 144

is theta, 144

the opinion of the viewpoint regulates the
consideration of the forms, their stillness
or their motion, and these considerations
consist of assignment of beauty or
ugliness to the forms and these
considerations alone are art, 157

being(s),

any being is a viewpoint; he is as much
a being as he is able to assume
viewpoints, 164

human beings are actually rather heroic and
noble characters, 300

human beings have a very high native sense of
justice, 268

many beings live lives of quiet correctness
without ever once making anything do
anything; things around them just
happen to be orderly; the social system
props them up, 354

on the way down don't believe they are
wrong, 311

way a being is hung with persistent
masses is the mechanism of getting
him to believe certain things are
undesirable, 404

beingness,

all the knowledge that's worth knowing is
outside your memory bank—in complete
and perfect contact with the beingness
that is you, 26

decision: the basic decision that life makes, that
theta makes, is "to be or not to be," 160

defined, 162

discipline of beingness is not necessarily the
limitation of beingness, 170

essence of true knowledge is the essence of
existing so that one can create beingness
and data to know, 15

first action of beingness is to assume a
viewpoint, 161

if you can be something you can certainly know
it; if you know something you can
certainly be it, 12

beingness, *(cont.)*

it is better to be able to decide and control a
few things to be, than to be under the
whip of an imagination which drives one
to be a great many things, none of which
are under one's control, 170

life is a unit energy source; that energy source *is*
the person, the personality, the center of
beingness, 109

limitation, rather than increase, of beingness is
the common course of existence, 173

person's ability to be is also his ability to
communicate, 173

reason behind beingness is the drama of cause
and effect, 163

there is no trick to being unless you spend your
time agreeing, 174

thetan can be what he can see, 172

whole business of knowingness is beingness, 12

bell tolls, one does not send to find for whom the
bell tolls without full willingness to have
tolled it and to have caused the cause of its
tolling, 471

betrayal, help is always betrayal to a thoroughly
aberrated person, 229

blame, if you blame somebody hard enough and
long enough, you have kept on electing them
as cause until they are much more powerful
than yourself, 464

body,

thetan is the person himself—not his body or
his name, the physical universe, his
mind, or anything else; that which is
aware of being aware; the identity which
is the individual, 117

today we live in a vast cult called "Worship the
body," 226

computation, *(cont.)*
>imagination is vital to computation, for it recombines for the purposes of creation, construction and prediction, 56
>is taking the maybes out of existence, 64
>worry is constant, irresolute computation—constant computation on a certain point or a certain problem, 73

confidence, ability to make one's way and, 233

confront,
>fear is an unwillingness to confront, 7
>handling of a problem seems to be simply the increase of ability to confront the problem, 373
>if one can confront, he can be aware, 14
>inability to confront evil leads people into disregarding it or discounting it or not seeing it at all, 277
>looking into the past and looking into the extreme future, alike, are efforts to avoid present time and efforts to look elsewhere than at something, 72
>lowest confront there is, is the confront of evil, 276

confusion, when you think of uncertainty, stupidity and insecurity, think of confusion and you'll have it down pat, 67

consciousness, too much agreement under duress brings about the vanishment of one's entire consciousness, 186

consideration,
>stupidity is the unknownness of consideration, 287
>theta can become a problem by its considerations, but then becomes MEST, 126

contribution, art is the result of integration of all its components; one can add that the result invites contribution of and from the beholder, 151

control,
>bad: disharmonious alignment, 460
>force, willingness and control, 249
>good: harmonious alignment, 460
>high-tone individual controls his environment, 315
>it is difficult to be responsible for something or control something unless you have *knowledge* of it, 29
>one of the control mechanisms which has been used on thetans is that when they rise in potential they are led to believe themselves one with the universe, 106
>power (defined as light-year kilotons per microsecond) of a thetan is measured by nothing else than the distance (defined as spherical spatial length) around him in his environment that he can control, 114
>so long as a natural phenomenon remains the knowledge of a few and is denied to the many it can be utilized to control the many, 36
>war and, 252, 253, 256
>when good sense and good judgment are not added into control, control gets a bad name, 467

counter-effort, so long as an organism can employ in its survival a counter-effort, that counter-effort is not aberrative, 428

courage,
>courage could be summed up in (1) being willing to cause something, and (2) going ahead to achieve the effect one has postulated against any and all odds, 366

evaluation, *(cont.)*

when a man tries to erect the plans of a
lifetime or a profession on data which he,
himself, has never evaluated, he cannot
possibly succeed, 24

evil,

inability to confront evil leads people into
disregarding it or discounting it or not
seeing it at all, 277

it is not evil to like yourself or love yourself, 198

lowest confront there is, is the confront
of evil, 276

man is evil only when he is aberrated, 298

whatever man consists of, he is basically *not*
evil; he is merely ignorant, 299

exchange, it is *exchange* which maintains the
inflow and outflow that gives a person
space around him and keeps the bank off of
him, 439

exert, man is solving himself to extinction; and all
on the slogan, "Don't exert yourself," 365

exhaustion, it is only when something makes
man unwilling, stops him too often and kills
his interest in what he is doing that he
becomes exhausted, 384

existence,

computation is taking the maybes out of
existence, 64

cycle of existence for theta consists of a
disorganized and painful smash into MEST
and then a withdrawal with a knowledge
of some of the laws of MEST, to come
back and smash into MEST again, 125

the limitation, rather than the increase, of
beingness is the common course of
existence, 173

existence, *(cont.)*

your enthusiasm and zest for existence comes
mainly from your ability to differentiate, 76

experience,

the more fixed the identity of the person may be,
the less the experience of which he is
capable, 176

there is an area of existence known as
experience—the willingness to
experience, 371

extinction, man is solving himself to
extinction, 365

fact,

logic is the gradient scale of relating facts one to
another, 79

something that can be proven to exist by visible
evidence, 80

failure,

dramatizing is an apology for failure, 171

if we cannot imagine eventualities, we cannot
prevent future failures, 50

faith,

man without an abiding faith is, by observation
alone, more of a thing than a man, 302

men without a strong and lasting faith in a
Supreme Being are less capable, less
ethical and less valuable to themselves
and society, 242

false data,

causes errors of computation, 288

road to ruin is paved with false
information, 288

fame, has at its end a completely fixed
identification which is timeless, but which
unfortunately is matter and which equally
unfortunately, is inaction, 176

family,
> government wishing to deprave its people destroys the family, 230
> group with the common goal of group survival and advancement, 204

fear,
> comes about with the loss of confidence in one's ability to make his way, 233
> inaction and indecision in the present is because of fear of consequences of the future, 51
> is a state of imperception, an unwillingness to confront, 7
> people do not acquire obsessively those things which they do not fear, 446

feat, what is a great feat; it's something that can't be duplicated, 441

feelings, a being causes his *own* feelings, 169

force,
> man cannot be controlled by force; man is controlled only by his own willingness, 249
> man's ability to handle destructive physical universe forces is far, far greater than his ability to handle himself, 248
> may win dominion and control but will never win acceptance and respect, 362
> reason and, 246
> state which uses force is doomed to failure, 257
> universe of force; not a universe of reason, 247

freedom,
> cannot be erased; a static cannot be as-ised, 105
> if you truly understand, then you will be truly free, 196
> in knowing what is thought right, what is thought wrong, 270

freedom, *(cont.)*
> least-free person is the person who cannot reveal his own acts and who protests the revelation of the improper acts of others, 272
> lessening of freedom, effect on a country, 225
> search for freedom is either the retreat from past failures to communicate or the effort to attain new communication, 189
> single men and determined groups have been the only makers of space in which man could walk free, 316

future,
> creative and constructive imaginings about the future are not untruths but are postulated new realities, 55
> every calculation of effort made by the mind is directed toward future, 78
> if a man has no goals he doesn't even have a future, 59
> inaction and indecision in the present is because of fear of consequences of the future, 51
> individual compares conditions in the past to observations in the present in order to calculate efforts in the future, 78
> looking into the past and looking into the extreme future, alike, are efforts to avoid present time and efforts to look elsewhere than at something, 72
> relationship with a member of the opposite sex and, 218

game(s),
> agreement to rules and penalties, 338
> complexity in a game, 342
> efficiency and inefficiency and, 370
> knowingness that they are games, 341

game(s), *(cont.)*

life is a game wherein theta as the static solves the problems of theta as MEST, 128

one can have a game and know it; he can be in a game and not know it; the difference is his determinism, 340

prize of winning is making a new game, 349

require space and havingness, 341

the more serious you take the game, the less chance there is of winning, 348

when done the player keeps around tokens, 344

game condition, it takes unknowingness, joined to a game condition, to bring about aberration, 68

genius, five morons do not make a genius, 304

goal,

a man is as well off as his goals and dreams are intact, 46

if a man can dream, if a man can have goals, he can be happy and he can be alive; if he has no goals he doesn't even have a future, 59

life is a series of attained goals, 426

god,

postulate of a god of a universe is effective in that universe, 92

there are gods above all other gods, and gods beyond the gods of universes, but it were better, far better, to be a raving madman in his cell than to be a thing with the ego, cruelty and jealous lust that base religions have set up to make men grovel down, 449

government, wishing to deprave its people, actions of, 230

gradient scale, death is actually a gradient scale, 415

great man, that man who can be a great man and at the same time assume every other viewpoint there is, is really a great man, 165

greatness,

does not stem from savage wars or being known, 258

stems from being true to one's decency, from going on helping others whatever they do or think or say and despite all savage acts against one, 258

group,

family is a group with the common goal of group survival and advancement, 204

ideal group member is capable of working causatively in full cooperation with his fellows in the achievement of group goals and the realization of his own happiness, 166

is as capable as it contains capable individual members, 243

never desert a group to which you owe your support, 239

primary human failing is an inability to function as himself or contribute to group achievements, 223

happiness,

is applied individual effort, 420

is important, 421

man is not happy unless he is honest; white, black, red or brown, 290

people seek happiness in various ways, hectically, seriously, desperately; but the odd part of it is that they find only what they themselves put there, 49

hat, when a person has no hat he lacks purpose and value, 377

knowingness, *(cont.)*

if you can be something you can certainly know it; if you know something you can certainly be it, 12

is being certainness, 4

it's part of wisdom to know what you don't know, 10

knowing how to know is definition of highest level of knowingness, 2

perception is knowing across a distance, 8

reduced by assuming one must be in certain places to perceive and so know, and that one cannot be in certain places, 7

reduced by assuming that one cannot know or knows wrongly, 5

static has the capability of total knowingness, 197

thetan is a knowingness, 3

thetan reduces his knowingness only to have action, 3

thought consists entirely of knowing and not-knowing and the shades of gray between, 63

total knowingness would consist of total ARC, 197

whole business of knowingness is beingness, 12

knowledge, *see also* **knowingness**

all the knowledge that's worth knowing is outside your memory bank—in complete and perfect contact with the beingness that is you, 26

any knowledge which can be sensed, measured, experienced, by any entity is capable of influencing that entity, 23

essence of true knowledge is the essence of existing so that one can create beingness and data to know, 15

knowledge, *(cont.)*

evolution of knowledge is toward simplicity, not complexity, 22

it is difficult to be responsible for something or control something unless you have *knowledge* of it, 29

so long as a natural phenomenon remains the knowledge of a few and is denied to the many it can be utilized to control the many, 36

there is no knowledge worth knowing that's in your memory bank, 26

laugh, force yourself to laugh and you'll soon find something to laugh about, 168

leader, is that one who emotionally affects others most strongly toward positive action, 435

learning, an evolution toward complexity is an evolution toward authoritarianism and pomposity—"You couldn't possibly understand this, therefore I, who pretend to, am important" is the attitude which mires learning, 35

life, *see also* **living(ness)**

all life is a repeating pulse and ebb and surge of motion, 150

attitude toward life makes every possible difference to our living, 425

becomes difficult when rhythmic prediction cannot occur, 150

communication is the heart of, 188

does not change so much as our attitude toward it, 425

evolves into a better condition by means of hard work, not by threats, 254

experience matter becomes havingness, 399

goal of, 124

life, *(cont.)*

    if you have the idea about *anything* you do that
        you just dabble in it, you will wind up
        with a dabble life, 422

    is a game wherein theta as the static solves the
        problems of theta as MEST, 128

    is a static which yet has the power of
        controlling, animating, mobilizing,
        organizing and destroying matter,
        energy and space and possibly even
        time, 105

    is a unit energy source; that energy source *is*
        the person, the personality, the center of
        beingness, 109

    is not much worth living if it cannot
        be enjoyed, 417

    knowing about life would also have to include
        knowing about death, 412

    never let it be said of you that you lived an
        amateur life, 422

    one can simply confront the whole thing, pain,
        misemotion, punishments, rewards and
        all and produce and exchange and learn
        to handle the administrative system he is
        in and himself administer his life and
        environ, 453

    people have to be told and kept in the frame of
        mind that life is worth living and that
        things are worth doing, 382

    series of attained goals, 426

    the persistency of the individual in life is directly
        governed by the strength of his basic
        dynamic, 359

    there is nothing to be gained by backing up
        from life, 423

    what of a person who can remember only
        this life, 414

life, *(cont.)*

    when one loses the illusion of one's dreams,
        when one no longer garbs one's
        none-too-brilliant history and rather
        perishable body with illusion, life, bluntly
        and brutally, isn't worth living, 96

life force, relationship with a member of the
    opposite sex and, 218

living(ness), *see also* **life**

    best expressed in terms of affinity, 184

    happiness is important, 421

    if this were all there were to surviving and if
        necessity were a vicious little gnome with
        a pitchfork, it seems rather obvious that
        there would be scant reason to go on
        living, 416

    is hot, it's fast, it's often brutal, 427

    life was busy teaching somebody a lesson, and
        the lesson it succeeded in teaching him
        was not to do any more living; and that
        ultimate lesson, then, was always at the
        base of education as it was done, so that
        education itself could be considered
        aberrative, 33

    no substitute for an all-out, over-the-ramparts,
        howling charge against life; that's
        living, 412

    one is as alive as he has space and as he can
        alter and occupy that space, 135

    third-dynamic activity for the most part, 222

logic,

    association is the essence of logic, 81

    concerns obtaining answers, 82

    gradient scale of relating facts one to
        another, 79

lose, one loses to the degree he is forbidden to
    have, 347

mass,
>object is mass, 116
>
>space or mass is no understanding, 116
>
>way a being is hung with persistent masses is the mechanism of getting him to believe certain things are undesirable, 404

mathematics, can be derived from ARC acting upon MEST, 200

matter,
>difference between thought and matter is that thought aligns in its highest echelon, and matter is chaos, 65
>
>entheta is just matter kicking up a final splatter, 133
>
>fame has at its end a completely fixed identification which is timeless, but which unfortunately is matter and which equally unfortunately, is inaction, 176
>
>from the standpoint of the MEST universe, the greatest reality would be had by matter itself and this seems to be its evident goal toward the thetan, to make him into solid energy, 98

maybe,
>as you go way up Tone Scale, you get less and less and less maybes, and you actually do less and less and less computing, and you do more and more and more knowing, 83
>
>can exist only in the presence of poor observation or the inability to observe, 6
>
>computation is taking the maybes out of existence, 64
>
>so long as you can remove maybes by the process of comparing data and get a situation which balances out yes or no, you are thinking smoothly, 64

maybe, *(cont.)*
>thought could be said to be the resolution of maybes, 63

MEST,
>could be considered to be under onslaught by theta, 127
>
>cycle of existence for theta consists of a disorganized and painful smash into MEST and then a withdrawal with a knowledge of some of the laws of MEST, to come back and smash into MEST again, 125
>
>is under raid; theta is doing the raiding, 127
>
>life is a game wherein theta as the static solves the problems of theta as MEST, 128
>
>man alone of the animal and vegetable kingdom possesses the potential power of changing MEST in wholesale lots into something theta can use, 130
>
>mathematics can be derived from ARC acting upon MEST, 200
>
>the purer the theta, the more MEST will be attracted under it, 131
>
>theta can become a problem by its considerations, but then becomes MEST, 126
>
>theta crushed too hard into MEST becomes entheta, 132
>
>way out of MEST ain't detest, 126

MEST universe, *see also* MEST
>from the standpoint of the MEST universe, the greatest reality would be had by matter itself and this seems to be its evident goal toward the thetan, to make him into solid energy, 98
>
>is found to consist of a high-level agreement amongst us, 90

observation, *(cont.)*
given a viewpoint and four, eight or more
points to view, one has space; space
is a problem of observation, not of
physics, 136
to obtain a certainty one must be able to
observe, 4

optimist, silly, 308

order,
one must act, one must preserve order and
decency, but one need not hate or seek
vengeance, 281
when you start to introduce order into anything,
disorder shows up and blows off, 357

overt act(s),
idea of not harming anything and helping
everything are alike rather mad, 279
insane are just one seething mass of overt acts
and withholds; and they are very
physically sick people, 274
man or woman who must must must become a
victim and depart is departing because of
his or her own overts and withholds, 275
product of irresponsibility on one or more of the
dynamics, 474

own, to own is to be able to see or touch or
occupy, 405

pain,
entire source of pain is an effort to abstain, 372
run any equation into which pain has entered
and it can be seen that it reduces down
to possible nonsurvival, 416
sensation of pain is actually a sensation of loss;
it is a loss of beingness, a loss of position
and awareness, 403

paradox, an immortal being striving to survive
presents immediately a paradox, 112

parents, goal of most parents is obedience;
obedience is apathy; most *bad* children
become good the moment you let them up
the Tone Scale, 213; *see also* **child(ren)**

past, looking into the past and looking into the
extreme future, alike, are efforts to avoid
present time and efforts to look elsewhere
than at something, 72

perception,
ability to think is the capability of the mind to
perceive, pose and resolve specific and
general problems, 74
any knowledge which can be sensed, measured,
experienced, by any entity is capable of
influencing that entity, 23
fear is a state of imperception, 7
if one is aware, he can perceive and act, 14
is knowing across a distance, 8
knowingness is reduced by assuming one must be
in certain places to perceive and so know,
and that one cannot be in certain places, 7
mechanics of perception consist of putting
something out there and then wondering
what it is, 8

persistence,
simply comes about through an inability to
create or destroy something, 408
the persistency of the individual in life is directly
governed by the strength of his basic
dynamic, 359
we can achieve a persistence only when we
mask a truth, 285

personal integrity, personal integrity is knowing
what you know, 11

personality, life is a unit energy source; that
energy source *is* the person, the personality,
the center of beingness, 109

Q and A, *(cont.)*
    people live Q-and-A lives, 378
    people who can get things done just don't
        Q-and-A, 391

randomity, one obtains randomity by abandoning
    responsibility in some sphere; he will then
    find himself in conflict in that sphere, 466

reality,
    creative and constructive imaginings about the
        future are not untruths but are postulated
        new realities, 55
    from the standpoint of the MEST universe, the
        greatest reality would be had by matter
        itself and this seems to be its evident goal
        toward the thetan, to make him into
        solid energy, 98
    is agreement, 186
    never compromise with your own reality, 187
    theta has as its primary manifestations affinity,
        reality and communication, 180
    understanding is composed of affinity, reality
        and communication, 195

reason,
    analytical waves are too coarse to attain theta's
        zero or infinity "wavelength"; art alone
        may do so, 147
    an individual cannot approach a future goal or
        even strongly postulate, 327
    ethics are reason, 262
    force and, 246
    prejudice and, 70
    you face force with reason and continue to apply
        reason, 360

reasoning,
    highest level of reasoning is complete
        differentiation, 75

reasoning, *(cont.)*
    lowest level of reasoning is complete inability to
        differentiate, which is to say,
        identification, 75
    theta acting upon MEST with affinity,
        communication and reality takes on an
        aspect known as reasoning or
        understanding, 200

relationship, human being does not seem to be
    complete without a relationship with a
    member of the opposite sex, 218

respect, arrogance and force may win dominion
    and control but will never win acceptance
    and respect, 362

responsibility,
    all real difficulty stems from no
        responsibility, 468
    area or sphere of influence the individual can
        rationally affect around other people, life,
        MEST, and the general environment, 470
    defined as the concept of being able to care for,
        to reach or to be, 461
    full responsibility is not fault; it is recognition of
        being cause, 462
    is the ability and willingness to assume the
        status of full source and cause for all
        efforts and counter-efforts on all
        dynamics, 459
    it is difficult to be responsible for something or
        control something unless you have
        knowledge of it, 29
    it is folly to try to control something or even know
        something without responsibility, 458
    keynote of responsibility is the willingness to
        handle energy, 460
    means "the determination of the *cause* which
        produced the *effect*," 451

responsibility, *(cont.)*

    one *becomes* that to which he assigns responsibility too often and too long; he makes it *cause* and, at last, to be cause himself, he must be the thing, 465

    one obtains randomity by abandoning responsibility in some sphere, 466

    slaves are made by giving them freedom from responsibility, 474

    soldier shot on the field of battle may "blame" the sniper, Selective Service, the stupidity of government, but he nevertheless had full responsibility, 463

    way not to have is to ignore or combat or withdraw from, 476

responsible, *see also* **responsibility**

    one is as *responsible* as one can *communicate,* 475

    to be responsible for something one does not actually have to care for it or reach it or be it; one only needs to believe or know that he has the ability to care for it, reach it or be it, 461

results, authoritarians do not achieve any results beyond their own satisfaction—which is not reason enough for the student or technician who wishes to get things done, 36

revolt, failure to provide jobs, purpose and training on jobs begets revolt, 385

revolution,

    man's wars, his revolutions, his suffering, all stem from his lack of data on the mind and man, 227

    no revolution ever won anything; life evolves into a better condition by means of hard work, not by threats, 254

right(ness),

    does not consist of being unwilling to harm, and being wrong does not consist only of not harming, 269

    justice could be called the adjudication of the relative rightness or wrongness of a decision or an action, 278

    man who has no impulse to set things right is insane, 364

    no absolute rights or absolute wrongs, 269

    person still possessed of some vigor will seek to be and always asserts that he is right, 310

rule, a good rule is one which aligns action and permits compliance, 339

sanity,

    basic definition of sanity in this somewhat nebulously learned society is whether or not a person agrees with everyone else, 45

    insane are just one seething mass of overt acts and withholds; and they are very physically sick people, 274

    person who is sane has a high ARC value, 199

    the less certain the individual on any subject, the less sane he could be said to be upon that subject, 66

science, every bit of scientific lore which has been accumulated by scientists in the hope that it may better the lot of their fellow men has eventually been employed in the destruction of men, 251

self-confidence, whole feeling of self-confidence and competence actually derives from one's ability to control or leave uncontrolled the various items and people in his surroundings, 442

self-determinism, *see also* **determinism**

> applied, will create, conserve, alter and possibly destroy universes, 99
>
> choice is the keynote of, 324
>
> common denominator of all life impulses, 322
>
> defined, 323
>
> essence of a man is his self-determinism, 322
>
> *nothing* which we do is beyond self-determined action, 332
>
> universes are created by the application of self-determinism on eight dynamics, 88
>
> we are all self-determined, natively, 332
>
> your self-determinism and your honor are more important than your immediate life, 330

self-satisfaction, doing things for self-satisfaction is for professors who can't, 155

sex, revulsion to sex inclines at last to slavery to sex, 447

silly optimist, 308

simplicity,

> evolution of knowledge is toward simplicity, not complexity, 22
>
> once upon a time there was a little thetan; and he was a happy little thetan and the world was a simple thing, 104
>
> people are always attempting to do more complicated things and consider this good; what people are doing, actually, is losing their ability to do simple things, 37

sin, misusing a counter-effort you have received, 268

situation, almost anyone, no matter his position, can remedy a situation no matter what's wrong if he or she really wants to, 358

slavery,

> attempts at enslavement arise primarily from fear, 233
>
> demonstrable law, not an opinion, that he who would enslave his fellows becomes himself enslaved, 302
>
> effect on a country, 225
>
> element necessary in order to bring about slavery, 232
>
> if governments and civilizations continue to produce things to convince people that they are just slaves and that things aren't worth doing and that they have to be pushed into work with a whip, the whole society degenerates, 389
>
> no society can exist on a fabric of slaves, 231
>
> slaves are made by giving them freedom from responsibility, 474
>
> when nobody knows and the rules are all "off the cuff," 270

smile, force yourself to smile and you'll soon stop frowning, 168

society,

> as a society declines, it more and more resorts to authoritarian teaching and attempts increasingly to impress upon the individual that he must adjust to his environment and that he cannot adjust his environment to him, 30
>
> building unit of a great society is the individual, 234
>
> can only survive when it is built by the shoulders and hands of willing men, 241
>
> declines in exact ratio to the contempt in which it holds pleasure and advances in ratio to the respect it has for pleasure, 235

theta, *(cont.)*

    courage might be considered the theta force
        necessary to overcome obstacles in
        surviving, 354

    crushed too hard into MEST becomes
        entheta, 132

    cycle of existence for theta consists of a
        disorganized and painful smash into MEST
        and then a withdrawal with a knowledge
        of some of the laws of MEST, to come
        back and smash into MEST again, 125

    favors an aesthetic band because that's closest in
        to motionlessness; it's closest in to the
        fine wavelength which can append to
        theta itself, 145

    greatest potentialities of, 201

    has as its primary manifestations affinity,
        reality and communication, 180

    it is an aspect of theta that the more it is
        enturbulated the easier it is to enter
        enturbulence into it, 134

    life is a game wherein theta as the static solves
        the problems of theta as MEST, 128

    man alone of the animal and vegetable kingdom
        possesses the potential power of changing
        MEST in wholesale lots into something
        theta can use, 130

    MEST could be considered to be under onslaught
        by theta, 127

    MEST is under raid; theta is doing the
        raiding, 127

    the purer the theta, the more MEST will be
        attracted under it, 131

    what wave most closely approximates theta? It
        would be one of nearly infinite smallness,
        and that wave is found to be aesthetic,
        the wavelength of the arts, 156

thetan, *see also* **theta**

    can be what he can see, 172

    do not, as they rise up the scale, merge with
        other individualities, 106

    first and foremost themselves, 107

    have the power of becoming anything they wish
        while still retaining their own
        individuality, 107

    immortal and is possessed of capabilities well in
        excess of those hitherto predicted for man, 111

    indestructible, 113

    individuals, 106

    is a knowingness, 3

    is no mass, 116

    is understanding, 116

    most familiar to one and all as *you*, 117

    most valuable thing he possesses, 338

    nothing can ever be done directly to a thetan; so
        the trick is, one has to attach him to a
        possession, and then hurt the possession, 115

    once upon a time there was a little thetan; and
        he was a happy little thetan and the
        world was a simple thing, 104

    one of the control mechanisms which has been
        used on thetans is that when they rise in
        potential they are led to believe
        themselves one with the universe, 106

    person himself—not his body or his name, the
        physical universe, his mind, or anything
        else; that which is aware of being aware;
        the identity which *is* the individual, 117

    power (defined as light-year kilotons per
        microsecond) of a thetan is measured
        by nothing else than the distance
        (defined as spherical spatial length)
        around him in his environment that he
        can control, 114

work, *(cont.)*

don't ever feel weaker because you work for
somebody stronger, 437

great revolutions occur out of a mass inability to
work, 388

has a purpose, 392

if all the workmen in America and England
became unwilling to work, one would
again see a barbarism, 394

if anything will kill Western society, it is either
tremendous political blunders which bring
about an atomic war, or this philosophy
that work is too hard to confront, 379

society almost demands that a man consider
whatever he is doing as work and
demands that he consider work as an
unhappy thing, 393

was seen to be something that was
arduous and necessary and therefore not
interesting, 392

work, *(cont.)*

where we have fault to find with working, it
grows out of our own fear that we will
not be permitted to continue work, 387

workability, *a datum or a formula or anything
like that is really just as good to an
individual as it's workable,* 21

worry, *is constant, irresolute computation—
constant computation on a certain point or a
certain problem,* 73

Worship the body, *today we live in a vast cult
called "Worship the body,"* 226

yourself,

in order to have an understanding of
yourself, you must have good ARC with
yourself, 198

it is not evil to like yourself or love yourself, 198

Bibliography

The quotes in this book were taken from the books, lectures, issues and articles by L. Ron Hubbard listed below. More data on the books and many of the lectures can be found on the following pages. For copies of these materials, contact any of the addresses given in the list at the back of this book.

Books:

Advanced Procedure and Axioms
All About Radiation
A New Slant on Life
Child Dianetics
Creation of Human Ability, The
Dianetics 55!
Dianetics: The Modern Science of Mental Health
Dynamics of Life, The
Handbook for Preclears
Have You Lived Before This Life?
Notes on the Lectures of L. Ron Hubbard
Problems of Work, The
Science of Survival

Scientology 8-80
Scientology 8-8008
Scientology: The Fundamentals of Thought
Self Analysis in Scientology

Organization Executive Course Issues:

Artistic Presentation	HCO PL 8 Oct. 64
Blow-Offs	HCO PL 31 Dec. 59R
Competence	HCO PL 4 Jan. 71
Conditions, How to Assign	HCO PL 20 Oct. 67
Ethics, the Design Of	HCO PL 7 Dec. 69 I
Good Workers	HCO PL 10 Aug. 64
Justice	HCO Exec Ltr 18 Mar. 65
Responsibility Again	HCO PL 17 Jan. 62 II
Supreme Test, The	HCO PL 19 Aug. 67

Management Series Issues:

Admin Know-How No. 30	HCO PL 1 Sept. 73
Anatomy of Thought, The Data Series 1R	HCO PL 26 Apr. 70R
Breakthroughs Data Series 3	HCO PL 12 May 70

Technical Bulletins

Students Who Succeed — HCOB 15 Nov. 72 II
Temperatures — HCOB 27 Jan. 72
Theory of Affinity, Reality and Communication, The — Dianetic Auditor's Bulletin, Feb. 51
Theta–MEST Theory Extended, The — ca. May 53
What the Thetan is Trying to Do — PAB 11, early Oct. 53

Personal Achievement Series Lectures:

Deterioration of Liberty
Differences Between Scientology and Other Studies
Operation Manual for the Mind
Power of Choice and Self-Determinism
Road to Truth, The

Lecture Series:

Perception of Truth Lectures, The
Philadelphia Doctorate Course Lectures, The
Power of Simplicity Lectures, The
Route to Infinity Lectures, The
Secret of the MEST Universe Lectures
Universes and the War Between Theta and MEST Lectures

Other Lectures:

Cause and Effect: Education, Unknowing Effect, 30 Dec. 57
   Ability Congress
Clear Procedure, 9 Dec. 57, *Ability Congress*
Dianetics 1961 and the Whole Solution to
   the Problems of the Human Mind, 1 Jan. 61
Field of Scientology, The, 1 Jan. 61

Articles and Research Notes:

"Ability Book"
"An Invitation to Freedom, Man *Can Save His Soul*"
"Auditor First Should Know Tools Before He Goes In for Artistic"
" 'Being Cause' Is Society's Major Aberration"
"Child Scientology"
"Communication"
"Dianetics: Its Relationship to Scientology"
"Dianometry, Your Ability and State of Mind"
"False Reports"
"Fast Justice"
"Fight for Freedom, The"
"Goal of Training, The"
"How Do People Know They Have Lived Before?"

"How to Study Scientology"
"Is It Possible to Be Happy?"
"Limitations of Homo Novis, The"
"Loophole in Guarded Rights, The"
"LRH Research Notes"
"Marital Scientology"
"Riots"
"Personal Integrity"
"Scientology's Future"
"SOP 8-C: The Rehabilitation of the Human Spirit"
"States of Existence, The"
"This Is Scientology, The Science of Certainty"
"What It Means to Be a Scientologist"

Books and Tapes
by L. Ron Hubbard

Understanding: The Universal Solvent

L. Ron Hubbard's works contain a wisdom which is extraordinary in its perception and power. *Understanding: The Universal Solvent* is a collection of quotations from those works containing over 450 quotes, fully categorized and indexed for ease of reading. This book covers, in concise, strikingly beautiful and often poetic form, some of the most basic truths in this universe.

Basic Scientology Books

The Basic Scientology Books Package contains the knowledge you need to be able to improve conditions in life. These books are available individually or as a set, complete with an attractive slipcase.

Scientology: The Fundamentals of Thought • Improve life and make a better world with this easy-to-read book that lays out the fundamental truths about life and thought. No such knowledge has ever before existed, and no such results have ever before been attainable as those which can be reached by the use of this knowledge. Equipped with this book, alone, one could perform seeming miracles in changing the states of health, ability and intelligence of people. This *is* how life works. This *is* how you change men, women and children for the better, and attain greater personal freedom.

A New Slant on Life • Have you ever asked yourself Who am I? What am I? This book of articles by L. Ron Hubbard answers these all-too-common questions. This is knowledge one can use every day— for a new, more confident and happier slant on life!

The Problems of Work • Work plays a big part in the game of life. Do you really enjoy your work? Are you certain of your job security? Would you like the increased personal satisfaction of doing your work well? This is the book that shows exactly how to achieve these things and more. The game of life—and within it, the game of work—can be enjoyable and rewarding.

Scientology 0-8: The Book of Basics • What is life? Did you know an individual can create space, energy and time? Here are the basics of life itself, and the secrets of becoming cause over any area of your life. Discover how you can use the data in this book to achieve your goals.

Basic Dictionary of Dianetics and Scientology • Compiled from the works of L. Ron Hubbard, this convenient dictionary contains the terms and expressions needed by anyone learning Dianetics and Scientology technology. And a *special bonus*—an easy-to-read Scientology organizing board chart that shows you who to contact for services and information at your nearest Scientology organization.

OT[1] Library Package

All the following books contain the knowledge of a spiritual being's relationship to this universe and how his abilities to operate successfully in it can be restored. You can get all of these books individually or in a set, complete with an attractive slipcase.

Scientology 8-80 • What are the laws of life? We are all familiar with physical laws such as the law of gravity, but what laws govern life and thought? L. Ron Hubbard answers the riddles of life and its goals in the physical universe.

Scientology 8-8008 • Get the basic truths about your nature as a spiritual being and your relationship to the physical universe around you. Here, L. Ron Hubbard describes procedures designed to increase your abilities to heights previously only dreamed of.

Scientology: A History of Man • A fascinating look at the evolutionary background and history of the human race—revolutionary concepts guaranteed to intrigue you and challenge many basic assumptions about man's true power, potential and abilities.

---

1. *OT*: abbreviation for *Operating Thetan*, a state of beingness. It is a being "at cause over matter, energy, space, time, form and life." *Operating* comes from "able to operate without dependency on things," and *Thetan* is the Greek letter *theta* (θ), which the Greeks used to represent *thought* or perhaps *spirit*, to which an *n* is added to make a noun in the modern style used to create words in engineering. It is also θ^n or "theta to the nth degree," meaning unlimited or vast.

The Creation of Human Ability• This book contains processes designed to restore the power of a thetan over his own postulates, to understand the nature of his beingness, to free his self-determinism and much, much more.

Basic Dianetics Books

The Basic Dianetics Books Package is your complete guide to the inner workings of the mind. You can get all of these books individually or in a set, complete with an attractive slipcase.

Dianetics: The Modern Science of Mental Health• Acclaimed as the most effective self-help book ever published. Dianetics technology has helped millions reach new heights of freedom and ability. Millions of copies are sold every year! Discover the source of mental barriers that prevent you from achieving your goals—and how to handle them!

The Dynamics of Life• Break through the barriers to your happiness. This is the first book Ron wrote detailing the startling principles behind Dianetics—facts so powerful they can change forever the way you look at yourself and your potentials. Discover how you can use the powerful basic principles in this book to blast through the barriers of your mind and gain full control over your success, future and happiness.

Self Analysis • The complete do-it-yourself handbook for anyone who wants to improve their abilities and success potential. Use the simple, easy-to-learn techniques in *Self Analysis* to build self-confidence and reduce stress.

Dianetics: The Evolution of a Science • It is estimated that we use less than ten percent of our mind's potential. What stops us from developing and using the full potential of our minds? *Dianetics: The Evolution of a Science* is L. Ron Hubbard's incredible story of how he discovered the reactive mind and how he developed the keys to unlock its secrets. Get this firsthand account of what the mind really is, and how you can release its hidden potential.

Dianetics Graduate Books

These books by L. Ron Hubbard give you detailed knowledge of how the mind works—data you can use to help yourself and others break out of the traps of life. While you can get these books individually, the Dianetics Graduate Books Package can also be purchased as a set, complete with an attractive slipcase.

Science of Survival • If you ever wondered why people act the way they do, you'll find this book a wealth of information. It's vital to anyone who wants to understand others and improve personal relationships. *Science of Survival* is built around a remarkable chart—the Hubbard Chart of Human Evaluation. With it you can understand and

predict other people's behavior and reactions and greatly increase your control over your own life. This is a valuable handbook that can make a difference between success and failure on the job and in life.

Dianetics 55! • Your success in life depends on your ability to communicate. Do you know a formula exists for communication? Learn the rules of better communication that can help you live a more fulfilling life. Here, L. Ron Hubbard deals with the fundamental principles of communication and how you can master these to achieve your goals.

Advanced Procedure and Axioms • For the *first* time the basics of thought and the physical universe have been codified into a set of fundamental laws, signaling an entirely new way to view and approach the subjects of man, the physical universe and even life itself.

Handbook for Preclears • Written as an advanced personal workbook, *Handbook for Preclears* contains easily done processes to help you overcome the effect of times you were not in control of your life, times that your emotions were a barrier to your success and much more. Completing all the fifteen auditing steps contained in this book sets you up for really being in *control* of your environment and life.

Child Dianetics • Here is a revolutionary new approach to rearing children with Dianetics auditing techniques. Find out how you can help your child achieve greater confidence, more self-reliance, improved learning rate and a happier, more loving relationship with you.

Notes on the Lectures of L. Ron Hubbard • *Compiled from his fascinating lectures given shortly after the publication of Dianetics, this book contains some of the first material Ron ever released on the ARC triangle and the Tone Scale, and how these discoveries relate to auditing.*

Basic Executive Books

The Basic Executive Books Package consists of the book The Problems of Work and the two books listed below. They are available individually or as a set, complete with an attractive slipcase.

How to Live Though an Executive • *What are the factors in business and commerce which, if lacking, can keep a person overworked and worried, keep labor and management at each other's throats, and make an unsafe working atmosphere? L. Ron Hubbard reveals principles based on years of research into many different types of organizations.*

Introduction to Scientology Ethics • *A complete knowledge of ethics is vital to anyone's success in life. Without knowing and applying the information in this book, success is only a matter of luck or chance. That is not much to look forward to. This book contains the answers to questions like, "How do I know when a decision is right or wrong?" "How can I predictably improve things around me?" The powerful ethics technology of L. Ron Hubbard is your way to ever-increasing survival.*

Purification Book Package

The books in the Purification Book Package contain data on the only effective way of handling drug and toxic residuals in the body, clearing the way for real mental and spiritual improvement—the Purification program. These books are available individually and as a specially boxed set.

Clear Body, Clear Mind: The Effective Purification Program. This book contains all the information on L. Ron Hubbard's Purification program. This is the only program of its kind in existence that has been found to clean the residues of drugs, toxins and elements harmful to human bodies out of them! Drugs and chemicals can stop a person's ability to improve himself or just to live life. This book describes the program which can make it possible to start living again.

Purification: An Illustrated Answer to Drugs. Presented in a concise, fully illustrated format, this book provides you with an overview of the Purification program. Our society is ridden by abuse of drugs, alcohol and medicine that reduce one's ability to think clearly. This book lays out what can be done about it, in a form which is easy for anyone to read and understand.

Purification Rundown Delivery Manual. This book is a manual which guides a person through the Purification Rundown step by step. It includes all of the needed reports as well as spaces for the person to write his successes and to attest to program completion. This manual makes administering the Purification Rundown simple and standard.

All About Radiation. Can the effects of radiation exposure be avoided or reduced? What exactly would happen in the event of an atomic explosion? Get the answers to these and many other questions in this illuminating book. *All About Radiation* describes observations and discoveries concerning the physical and mental effects of radiation and the possibilities for handling them. Get the real facts on the subject of radiation and its effects.

Other Scientology Books

Have You Lived Before This Life?. This is the book that sparked a flood of interest in the ancient puzzle: Does man live only one life? The answer lay in mystery, buried until L. Ron Hubbard's researches unearthed the truth. Actual case histories of people recalling past lives in auditing tell the tale.

Background and Ceremonies of the Church of Scientology. Discover the beautiful and inspiring ceremonies of the Church of Scientology, and its fascinating religious and historical background. This book contains the illuminating Creed of the Church, church services, sermons and ceremonies, many as originally given in person by L. Ron Hubbard, Founder of Scientology.

What Is Scientology? • Scientology applied religious philosophy has attracted great interest and attention since its beginning. What is Scientology philosophy? What can it accomplish—and why are so many people from all walks of life proclaiming its effectiveness? Find the answers to these questions and many others in *What Is Scientology?*

Dianetics and Scientology Technical Dictionary • This dictionary is your indispensable guide to the words and ideas of Scientology and Dianetics technologies—technologies which can help you increase your know-how and effectiveness in life. Over three thousand words are defined—including a new understanding of vital words like *life, love* and *happiness* as well as Scientology terms.

Modern Management Technology Defined: Hubbard Dictionary of Administration and Management • Here's a real breakthrough in the subject of administration and management! Eighty-six hundred words are defined for greater understanding of any business situation. Clear, precise Scientology definitions describe many previously baffling phenomena and bring truth, sanity and understanding to the often murky field of business management.

Organization Executive Course • The *Organization Executive Course* volumes contain organizational technology never before known to

man. This is not just how a Scientology organization works; this is how the operation of *any* organization, *any* activity, can be improved. A person knowing the data in these volumes fully, and applying it, could completely reverse any downtrend in a company—or even a country!

Management Series Volumes 1, 2 and 3 • These books contain technology that anyone who works with management in any way must know completely to be a true success. Contained in these books are such subjects as data evaluation, the technology of how to organize any area for maximum production and expansion, how to handle personnel, the actual technology of public relations and much more.

Introductory and Demonstration Processes and Assists • How can you help someone increase his enthusiasm for living? How can you improve someone's self-confidence on the job? Here are basic Scientology processes you can use to help others deal with life and living.

Volunteer Minister's Handbook • This is a big, practical how-to-do-it book to give a person the basic knowledge on how to help self and others through the rough spots in life. It consists of twenty-one sections—each one covering important situations in life, such as drug and alcohol problems, study difficulties, broken marriages, accidents and illnesses, a failing business, difficult children, and much more. This is the basic tool you need to help someone out of troubles, and bring about a happier life.

Research and Discovery Series • These volumes contain the only existing day-to-day, week-to-week record of the progress of L. Ron Hubbard's research in Dianetics and Scientology. Through the pages of these beautiful volumes you follow L. Ron Hubbard's fantastic research adventure, beginning in the depths of man's degradation and obsession with the material universe and soaring to the realms of the spirit, freed from the bondage of the past.

Technical Bulletins • These volumes contain all of L. Ron Hubbard's technical bulletins and issues from the earliest to the latest. Almost any technical question can be answered from the pages of these volumes, which also include an extremely extensive master subject index.

The Personal Achievement Series

There are nearly three thousand recorded lectures by L. Ron Hubbard on the subjects of Dianetics and Scientology. What follows is a sampling of these lectures, each known and loved the world over. All of these are presented in Clearsound state-of-the-art sound-recording technology, notable for its clarity and brilliance of reproduction.

Get all the Personal Achievement Series cassettes by L. Ron Hubbard listed below and ask your nearest Scientology church or organization or the publisher about future releases.

The Story of Dianetics and Scientology • In this lecture,

L. Ron Hubbard shares with you his earliest insights into human nature and gives a compelling and often humorous account of his experiences. Spend an unforgettable time with Ron as he talks about the start of Dianetics and Scientology!

The Road to Truth. The road to truth has eluded man since the beginning of time. In this classic lecture, L. Ron Hubbard explains what this road actually is and why it is the only road one MUST travel all the way once begun. This lecture reveals the only road to higher levels of living.

Scientology and Effective Knowledge. Voyage to new horizons of awareness! *Scientology and Effective Knowledge* by L. Ron Hubbard can help you understand more about yourself and others. A fascinating tale of the beginnings of Dianetics and Scientology.

The Deterioration of Liberty. What do governments fear so much in a population that they amass weapons to defend themselves from people? Find out from Ron in this classic lecture.

Power of Choice and Self-Determinism. Man's ability to determine the course of his life depends on his ability to exercise his power of choice. Find how you can increase your power of choice and self-determinism in life from Ron in this lecture.

Scientology and Ability. Ron points out that this universe is here because we perceive it and agree to it. Applying Scientology principles to life can bring new adventure to life and put you on the road to discovering better beingness.

The Hope of Man. Various men in history brought forth the idea that there was hope of improvement. But L. Ron Hubbard's discoveries in Dianetics and Scientology have made that hope a reality. Find out by listening to this lecture how Scientology has become man's one, true hope for his final freedom.

The Dynamics. In this lecture Ron gives incredible data on the dynamics: how man creates on them, what happens when a person gets stuck in just one, how wars relate to the third dynamic and much more.

Money. Ron talks in this classic lecture about that subject which makes or breaks men with the greatest of ease—money. Find out what money really is and gain greater control over your own finances.

Formulas for Success—*The Five Conditions.* How does one achieve real success? It sometimes appears that luck is the primary factor, but the truth of the matter is that natural laws exist which govern the conditions of life. These laws have been discovered by Ron, and in this lecture he gives you the exact steps to take in order to improve conditions in any aspect of your life.

Health and Certainty. You need certainty of yourself in order to achieve the success you want in life. In *Health and Certainty,*

L. Ron Hubbard tells how you can achieve certainty and really be free to think for yourself. Get this tape now and start achieving your full potential!

Operation Manual for the Mind • Everybody has a mind—but who has an operation manual for it? This lecture reveals why man went on for thousands of years without understanding how his mind is supposed to work. The problem has been solved. Find out how with this tape.

Miracles • Why is it that man often loses to those forces he resists or opposes? Why can't an individual simply overcome obstacles in life and win? In the tape lecture *Miracles*, L. Ron Hubbard describes why one suffers losses in life. He also describes how a person can experience the miracles of happiness, self-fulfillment and winning at life. Get a copy today.

The Road to Perfection—*The Goodness of Man* • Unlike earlier practices that sought to "improve" man because he was "bad," Scientology assumes that you have *good* qualities that simply need to be increased. In *The Road to Perfection*, L. Ron Hubbard shows how workable this assumption really is—and how you can begin to use your mind, talents and abilities to the fullest. Get this lecture and increase your ability to handle life.

The Dynamic Principles of Existence • What does it take to survive in today's world? It's not something you learn much about in school. You have probably gotten a lot of advice about how to "get along." Your survival right now is limited by the data you were given. This lecture describes the dynamic principles of existence, and tells how you can use these principles to increase your success in all areas of life. Happiness and self-esteem can be yours. Don't settle for anything less.

Man: Good or Evil? • In this lecture, L. Ron Hubbard explores the greatest mystery that has confronted modern science and philosophy—the true nature of man's livingness and beingness. Is man simply a sort of wind-up doll or clock—or worse, an evil beast with no control of his cravings? Or is he capable of reaching higher levels of ability, awareness and happiness? Get this tape and find out the *real* answers.

Differences between Scientology and Other Studies • The most important questions in life are the ones you started asking as a child: What happens to a person when he dies? Is man basically good, or is he evil? What are the intentions of the world toward me? Did my mother and father really love me? What is love? Unlike other studies, which try to *force* you to think a certain way, Scientology enables you to find your own answers. Listen to this important lecture. It will put you on the road to true understanding and belief in yourself.

The Machinery of the Mind • We do a lot of things "automatically"—such as driving a car. But what happens when a person's mental machinery takes over and starts running him? In this

fascinating lecture, L. Ron Hubbard gives you an understanding of what mental machinery really is, and how it can cause a person to lose control. You *can* regain your power of decision and be in full control of your life. Listen to this lecture and find out how.

The Affinity-Reality-Communication Triangle. Have you ever tried to talk to an angry man? Have you ever tried to get something across to someone who is really in fear? Have you ever known someone who was impossible to cheer up? Listen to this fascinating lecture by L. Ron Hubbard and learn how you can use the affinity-reality-communication triangle to resolve personal relationships. By using the data in this lecture, you can better understand others and live a happier life.

Increasing Efficiency. Inefficiency is a major barrier to success. How can you increase your efficiency? Is it a matter of changing your diet, or adjusting your working environment? These approaches have uniformly failed, because they overlook the most important element: *you.* L. Ron Hubbard has found those factors that *can* increase your efficiency, and he reveals it in this timely lecture. Get *Increasing Efficiency* now, and start achieving *your* full potential.

Man's Relentless Search. For countless centuries, man has been trying to find himself. Why does this quest repeatedly end in frustration and disappointment? What is he *really* looking for, and why can't he find it? For the real truth about man and life, listen to this

taped lecture by L. Ron Hubbard, *Man's Relentless Search*. Restore your belief in yourself!

Advanced Scientology Cassettes

The Philadelphia Doctorate Course Lectures • This series of incomparable lectures, given by L. Ron Hubbard in Philadelphia in December 1952, tore the lid off the secrets of this universe. They reveal what you can do as a spiritual being who is superior to matter, energy, space and time.

The Route to Infinity Lectures • In these seven lectures, Ron bridges the gap between the ideal and the current scene—including data to help you create your future the way you want it.

The Phoenix Lectures • In this profound series of twenty-eight lectures, Ron presents the truth of man's nature as a spiritual being and his existence in the physical universe. Ron goes over the famous Axioms of Scientology in detail. He also covers time, the conditions of existence, the track of traditional wisdom on the planet and much more.

More advanced books and lectures are available. Contact your nearest organization or write directly to the publisher for a full catalog.

For more information about Scientology or to order books and cassettes

Call: 1-800-334-LIFE
in the US and Canada

Is there such a thing as a hot line that doesn't believe in giving advice? What about a hot line for able individuals to help them solve their *own* problems?

"If we take a man and keep giving him advice," L. Ron Hubbard has said, "we don't necessarily wind up with a resolution of his problems. But if, on the other hand, we put him in a position where he had higher intelligence, where his reaction time was better, where he could confront life better, where he could identify the factors in his life more easily, then he's in a position where he can solve his own problems."

Call the unique new hot line and referral service with operators trained in Scientology technology. Callers find someone they can trust to talk to about a problem, and they are referred to their nearest Scientology church or organization for more information if they are interested.

You can also order books and cassettes by L. Ron Hubbard by calling this number.

Call this toll-free number
7 days a week
from 9 A.M. to 11 P.M. Pacific Standard Time.

Get Your Free Catalog
of Knowledge on
How to Improve Life

L. Ron Hubbard's books and tapes increase your ability to understand yourself and others. His works give you the practical know-how you need to improve your life and the lives of your family and friends.

Many more materials by L. Ron Hubbard are available than have been covered in the pages of this book. A free catalog of these materials is available on request.

Write for your free catalog today!

Bridge Publications, Inc.
4751 Fountain Avenue
Los Angeles, California 90029

NEW ERA Publications International ApS
Store Kongensgade 55
1264 Copenhagen K, Denmark

"I am always happy to hear from my readers."
L. Ron Hubbard

These were the words of L. Ron Hubbard, who was always very interested in hearing from his friends and readers. He made a point of staying in communication with everyone he came in contact with over his fifty-year career as a professional writer, and he had thousands of fans and friends that he corresponded with all over the world.

The publishers of L. Ron Hubbard's works wish to continue this tradition and welcome letters and comments from you, his readers, both old and new.

Additionally, the publishers will be happy to send you information on anything you would like to know about Ron, his extraordinary life and accomplishments and the vast number of books he has written.

Any message addressed to the Author's Affairs Director at Bridge Publications will be given prompt and full attention.

Bridge Publications, Inc.
1751 Fountain Avenue
Los Angeles, California 90029
USA

Church and Organization Address List

United States of America

Albuquerque
Church of Scientology
8106 Menaul Blvd., NE
Albuquerque, New Mexico 87110

Ann Arbor
Church of Scientology
122 S. Main, Suite 160
Ann Arbor, Michigan 48106

Atlanta
Church of Scientology
2632 Piedmont Rd., NE
Atlanta, Georgia 30324

Austin
Church of Scientology
2200 Guadalupe
Austin, Texas 78705

Boston
Church of Scientology
448 Beacon Street
Boston, Massachusetts 02115

Buffalo
Church of Scientology
47 West Huron Street
Buffalo, New York 14202

Chicago
Church of Scientology
3011 North Lincoln Avenue
Chicago, Illinois 60657

Cincinnati
Church of Scientology
215 West 4th Street, 5th Floor
Cincinnati, Ohio 45202

Clearwater
Church of Scientology
Flag® Service Organization
210 South Fort Harrison Avenue
Clearwater, Florida 34616

Columbus
Church of Scientology
167 East State Street
Columbus, Ohio 43215

Dallas
Church of Scientology
Celebrity Centre® Dallas
8501 Manderville Lane
Dallas, Texas 75231

Denver
Church of Scientology
375 South Navajo Street
Denver, Colorado 80223

Detroit
Church of Scientology
321 Williams Street
Royal Oak, Michigan 48067

Honolulu
Church of Scientology
1 N. King St., Lower Level
Honolulu, Hawaii 96817

Kansas City
Church of Scientology
3619 Broadway
Kansas City, Missouri 64111

Las Vegas
Church of Scientology
846 East Sahara Avenue
Las Vegas, Nevada 89104

Church of Scientology
Celebrity Centre Las Vegas
1100 South 10th Street
Las Vegas, Nevada 89104

Long Island
Church of Scientology
330 Fulton Avenue
Hempstead, New York 11550

Los Angeles and vicinity

Church of Scientology
4810 Sunset Boulevard
Los Angeles, California 90027

Church of Scientology
1451 Irvine Boulevard
Tustin, California 92680

Church of Scientology
263 East Colorado Boulevard
Pasadena, California 91101

Church of Scientology
10335 Magnolia Boulevard
North Hollywood, California 91601

Church of Scientology
American Saint Hill Organization
1413 North Berendo Street
Los Angeles, California 90027

Church of Scientology
American Saint Hill Foundation
1413 North Berendo Street
Los Angeles, California 90027

Church of Scientology
Advanced Organization of
   Los Angeles
1306 North Berendo Street
Los Angeles, California 90027

Church of Scientology
Celebrity Centre International
5930 Franklin Avenue
Hollywood, California 90028

Miami

Church of Scientology
120 Giralda Avenue
Coral Gables, Florida 33134

Minneapolis

Church of Scientology
1011 Nicollet Mall
Minneapolis, Minnesota 55403

Mountain View

Church of Scientology
2483 Old Middlefield Way
Mountain View, California, 94043

New Haven

Church of Scientology
909 Whalley Avenue
New Haven, Connecticut 06515

New York City

Church of Scientology
227 West 46th Street
New York City, New York 10036

Church of Scientology
Celebrity Centre New York
65 East 82nd Street
New York City, New York 10028

Orlando

Church of Scientology
710-A East Colonial Drive
Orlando, Florida 32803

Philadelphia

Church of Scientology
1315 Race Street
Philadelphia, Pennsylvania 19107

Phoenix

Church of Scientology
4450 North Central Avenue
Suite 102
Phoenix, Arizona 85012

Portland

Church of Scientology
323 SW Washington
Portland, Oregon 97204

Church of Scientology
Celebrity Centre Portland
709 Southwest Salmon Street
Portland, Oregon 97205

Sacramento

Church of Scientology
825 15th Street
Sacramento, California 95814

Salt Lake City

Church of Scientology
1931 S. 1100 East
Salt Lake City, Utah 84106

San Diego

Church of Scientology
701 "C" Street
San Diego, California 92101

San Francisco

Church of Scientology
83 McAllister Street
San Francisco, California 94102

San Jose

Church of Scientology
80 E. Rosemary
San Jose, California 95112

Santa Barbara

Church of Scientology
524 State Street
Santa Barbara, California 93101

Seattle

Church of Scientology
2603 3rd Street
Seattle, Washington 98121

St. Louis

Church of Scientology
9510 Page Boulevard
St. Louis, Missouri 63132

Tampa

Church of Scientology
4809 North Armenia Avenue
Suite 215
Tampa, Florida 33603

Washington, DC

Founding Church of Scientology
2125 "S" Street NW
Washington, DC 20008

Canada

Edmonton

Church of Scientology
10349 82nd Avenue
Edmonton, Alberta
Canada T6E 1Z9

Kitchener

Church of Scientology
8 Water Street North
Kitchener, Ontario
Canada N2H 5A5

Montréal

Church of Scientology
4489 Papineau Street
Montréal, Québec
Canada H2H 1T7

Ottawa

Church of Scientology
150 Rideau Street, 2nd Floor
Ottawa, Ontario
Canada K1N 5X6

Québec

Church of Scientology
350 Bd Chareste Est
Québec, Québec
Canada G1K 3H5

Toronto

Church of Scientology
696 Yonge Street, 2nd Floor
Toronto, Ontario
Canada M4Y 2A7

Vancouver

Church of Scientology
401 West Hastings Street
Vancouver, British Columbia
Canada V6B 1L5

Winnipeg

Church of Scientology
Suite 125–388 Donald Street
Winnipeg, Manitoba
Canada R3B 2J4

United Kingdom

Birmingham

Church of Scientology
60/62 Constitution Hill
Birmingham
England B19 3JT

Brighton

Church of Scientology
Dukes Arcade, Top Floor
Dukes Street
Brighton, Sussex
England BN1 1AG

East Grinstead

Saint Hill Foundation
Saint Hill Manor
East Grinstead, West Sussex
England RH19 4JY

Advanced Organization Saint Hill
Saint Hill Manor
East Grinstead, West Sussex
England RH19 4JY

Edinburgh

Hubbard Academy of Personal
   Independence
20 Southbridge
Edinburgh, Scotland EH1 1LL

London

Church of Scientology
68 Tottenham Court Road
London, England W1P 0BB

Manchester

Church of Scientology
258 Deansgate
Manchester, England M3 4BG

Plymouth

Church of Scientology
41 Ebrington Street
Plymouth, Devon
England PL4 9AA

Sunderland

Church of Scientology
51 Fawcett Street
Sunderland, Tyne and Wear
England SR1 1RS

Austria

Vienna

Church of Scientology
Schottenfeldgasse 13–15
1070 Vienna, Austria

Church of Scientology
Celebrity Centre Vienna
Senefeldergasse 11/5
1100 Vienna, Austria

Belgium

Brussels

Church of Scientology
45A, rue de l'Ecuyer
1000 Bruxelles, Belgium

Denmark

Aarhus

Church of Scientology
Guldsmedegade 17, 2
8000 Aarhus C, Denmark

Copenhagen
Church of Scientology
Store Kongensgade 55
1264 Copenhagen K, Denmark

Church of Scientology
Vesterbrogade 66
1620 Copenhagen V, Denmark

Church of Scientology
Advanced Organization Saint Hill
    for Europe and Africa
Jernbanegade 6
1608 Copenhagen V, Denmark

France

Angers
Church of Scientology
10–12, rue Max Richard
49000 Angers, France

Clermont-Ferrand
Church of Scientology
2 Pte rue Giscard de la Tour Fondue
63000 Clermont-Ferrand, France

Lyon
Church of Scientology
3, place des Capucins
69001 Lyon, France

Paris
Church of Scientology
65, rue de Dunkerque
75009 Paris, France

Church of Scientology
Celebrity Centre Paris
69, rue Legendre
75017 Paris, France

St. Etienne
Church of Scientology
24, rue Marengo
42000 St. Etienne, France

Germany

Berlin
Church of Scientology e.V.
Sponholzstrasse 51/52
1000 Berlin 41, Germany

Düsseldorf
Church of Scientology
Friedrichstrasse 28
4000 Düsseldorf, West Germany

Church of Scientology
Celebrity Centre Düsseldorf
Grupellostr. 28
4000 Düsseldorf, West Germany

Frankfurt
Church of Scientology
Darmstädter Landstrasse 213
6000 Frankfurt 70, West Germany

Hamburg
Church of Scientology e.V.
Steindamm 63
2000 Hamburg 1, West Germany

Church of Scientology
Celebrity Centre Hamburg
Mönckebergstrasse 5/IV
2000 Hamburg 1, West Germany

Hannover
Church of Scientology
Hubertusstrasse 2
D-3000 Hannover 1, West Germany

München
Church of Scientology e.V.
Beichstrasse 12
D-8000 München 40, West Germany

Stuttgart
Church of Scientology
Hirschstrasse 27
7000 Stuttgart 1, West Germany

Israel

Tel Aviv
Scientology and Dianetics College
7 Salomon Street
Tel Aviv 66023, Israel

Italy

Brescia
Church of Scientology
Dei Tre Laghi
Via Fratelli Bronzetti, 20
25125 Brescia, Italy

Catania
Church of Scientology
Via Giuseppe Garibaldi, 9
95121 Catania, Italy

Milano
Church of Scientology
Via Abetone, 10
20137 Milano, Italy

Monza
Church of Scientology
Via Cavour, 5
20052 Monza, Italy

Novara
Church of Scientology
Corso Cavallotti, 7
28100 Novara, Italy

Nuoro
Church of Scientology
Via G. Deledda, 43
08100 Nuoro, Italy

Padova
Church of Scientology
Via Mameli, 1/5
35131 Padova, Italy

Pordenone
Church of Scientology
Via Montereale, 10/C
33170 Pordenone, Italy

Roma
Church of Scientology
Via di San Vito, 11
00185 Roma, Italy

Torino
Church of Scientology
Via Guarini, 4
10121 Torino, Italy

Verona
Church of Scientology
Vicolo Chiodo, 4/A
37121 Verona, Italy

Netherlands

Amsterdam
Church of Scientology
Nieuwe Zijds Voorburgwal 271
1012 RL Amsterdam, Netherlands

Norway

Oslo
Church of Scientology
Storgata 9
0155 Oslo 1, Norway

Portugal

Lisbon
Instituto de Dianética
Rua Actor Taborda 39–4°
1000 Lisboa, Portugal

Spain

Barcelona
Dianética
Calle Pau Claris 85, Principal 1ª
08010 Barcelona, Spain

Madrid
Asociación Civil de Dianética
Montera 20, Piso 1° DCHA
28013 Madrid, Spain

Sweden

Göteborg
Church of Scientology
Odinsgatan 8
411 03 Göteborg, Sweden

Malmö
Church of Scientology
Simrishamnsgatan 10
21423 Malmö, Sweden

Stockholm
Church of Scientology
Kammakargatan 46
S-111 60 Stockholm, Sweden

Switzerland

Basel
Church of Scientology
Herrengrabenweg 56
4054 Basel, Switzerland

Bern
Church of Scientology
Schulhausgasse 12
3113 Rubigen
Bern, Switzerland

Genève
Church of Scientology
9 Route de Saint-Julien
1227 Carouge
Genève, Switzerland

Lausanne
Church of Scientology
10, rue de la Madeleine
1003 Lausanne, Switzerland

Zürich
Church of Scientology
Badenerstrasse 294
CH-8004 Zürich, Switzerland

Australia

Adelaide
Church of Scientology
24 Waymouth Street
Adelaide, South Australia 5000
Australia

Brisbane
Church of Scientology
2nd Floor, 106 Edward Street
Brisbane, Queensland 4000
Australia

Canberra
Church of Scientology
Suite 16, 108 Bunda Street
Civic Canberra
A.C.T. 2601, Australia

Melbourne
Church of Scientology
44 Russell Street
Melbourne, Victoria 3000
Australia

Perth
Church of Scientology
39–41 King Street
Perth, Western Australia 6000
Australia

Sydney
Church of Scientology
201 Castlereagh Street
Sydney, New South Wales 2000
Australia

Church of Scientology
Advanced Organization Saint Hill
   Australia, New Zealand and
   Oceania
19–37 Greek Street
Glebe, New South Wales 2037
Australia

Japan

Tokyo

Scientology Organization
101 Toyomi Nishi Gotanda Heights
2-13-5 Nishi Gotanda
Shinagawa-ku
Tokyo, Japan 141

New Zealand

Auckland

Church of Scientology
32 Lorne Street
Auckland 1, New Zealand

Africa

Bulawayo

Church of Scientology
74 Abercorn Street
Bulawayo, Zimbabwe

Cape Town

Church of Scientology
5 Beckham Street
Gardens
Cape Town 8001, South Africa

Durban

Church of Scientology
57 College Lane
Durban 4001, South Africa

Harare

Church of Scientology
First Floor State Lottery Building
PO Box 3524
Corner Speke Avenue and
   Julius Nyerere Way
Harare, Zimbabwe

Johannesburg

Church of Scientology
Security Building, 2nd Floor
95 Commissioner Street
Johannesburg 2001, South Africa

Church of Scientology
101 Huntford Building
40 Hunter Street
Cnr. Hunter and Fortesque Roads
Yeoville 2198
Johannesburg, South Africa

Port Elizabeth

Church of Scientology
2 St. Christopher
27 Westbourne Road
Central
Port Elizabeth 6001, South Africa

Pretoria

Church of Scientology
1st Floor City Centre
272 Pretorius Street
Pretoria 0002, South Africa

Latin America

Colombia

Bogotá

Centro Cultural de Dianética
Carrera 19 No. 39–55
Apartado Aereo 92419
Bogotá, D.E. Colombia

Mexico

Guadalajara

Organización Cultural Dianética de
   Guadalajara, A.C.
Av. Lopez Mateos Nte. 329
Sector Hidalgo
Guadalajara, Jalisco,
México

Mexico City

Asociación Cultural Dianética, A.C.
Hermes No. 46
Colonia Crédito Constructor
03940 México, D.F.

Instituto de Filosofía Aplicada, A.C.
Durango #105
Colonia Roma
06700 México, D.F.

Instituto de Filosofía Aplicada, A.C.
Plaza Rio de Janeiro No. 52
Colonia Roma
06700 México, D.F.

Instituto Technologico de
   Dianética, A.C.
Londres 38-5to piso
Colonia Juarez
C.P. 06600 México, D.F.

Organización, Desarrollo y
   Dianética, A.C.
Providencia 1000
Colonia Del Valle
C.P. 03100 México, D.F.

Centro de Dianética Polanco
Insurgentes Sur 536, 1er piso
   Esq. Nogales
Colonia Roma Sur
C.P. 06700 México, D.F.

Venezuela

Valencia
Asociación Cultural Dianética de
  Venezuela, A.C.
Avenida 101 No. 150–23
Urbanizacion La Alegria
Apartado Postal 833
Valencia, Venezuela

To obtain any books or cassettes by L. Ron Hubbard which are not available at your local organization, contact any of the following publishers:

Bridge Publications, Inc.
4751 Fountain Avenue
Los Angeles, California 90029

Continental Publications Liaison
  Office
696 Yonge Street
Toronto, Ontario
Canada M1Y 2A7

NEW ERA Publications
  International ApS
Store Kongensgade 55
1264 Copenhagen K, Denmark

Era Dinámica Editores,
S.A. de C.V.
Nicolás San Juan No. 208
Col. Del Valle
C.P. 03020 México, D.F.

NEW ERA Publications, Ltd.
78 Holmethorpe Avenue
Redhill, Surrey RH1 2NL
England

N.E. Publications Australia Pty. Ltd.
2 Verona Street
Paddington, New South Wales 2021
Australia

Continental Publications Pty. Ltd.
PO Box 27080
Benrose
2011 South Africa

NEW ERA Publications Italia Srl
Via L.G. Columella, 12
20128 Milano, Italy

NEW ERA Publications GmbH
Otto—Hahn—Strasse 25
6072 Dreieich 1, Germany

NEW ERA Publications France
111, boulevard de Magenta
75010 Paris, France

New Era Publications España, S.A.
C/De la Paz, 4/1° DCHA
28012 Madrid, Spain

New Era Publications Japan, Inc.
5-4-5-803 Nishi Gotanda
Shinagawa-ku
Tokyo, Japan 141